In Any
Given Room

Stories on the Indian Experience

I. D. Kapur

PROSPECT STREET PRESS

I. D. Kapur/Prospect Street Press

www.idkapur.com

Publisher's Note: This is a work of imagination and
memory. It reflects the author's recollections of
experiences over time. Some names and characteristics
have been changed and some events and dialogue have
been recreated.

In Any Given Room/I. D. Kapur -- 1st ed.
ISBN-13 978-0-9996259-6-5

Cover design: Karen Phillips /www.PhillipsCovers.com

To Gopal, Jennifer, and Raj,
for everything

In memory of Sid Salinger,
the first to believe

Contents

Foreword

We were traveling in an open *autorickshaw* one cold and foggy morning to grab a cup of coffee. I suddenly felt warm, and it was Indra's shawl that she shared even though I hadn't uttered a word. I fondly remember meeting her first on Diwali (festival of lights). She asked if I'd like to come along as she and Gopal took fireworks to the girl's orphanage in Patiala. The girls and Indra could communicate comfortably despite not speaking each other's language because Indra had a very high EQ.

One of the greatest gifts from someone is making you feel relatable and vital, and that is what my dear friend, Indra, is about to me. When she feels something, she acts on it and, more importantly, finishes it with perfection and always makes it look easy.

I admire how Indra structurally explains simple life experiences so that even the mundane things feel essential and relatable. I'm confident that this collection of stories embracing five decades of social challenges, cultural minefields, lasting friendships, and deep love for India will be an excellent experience for the reader.

Dr. Pooja Walia Bedi, Delhi, India

Glossary of Hindi Words

Arranged Marriage	Parents choose a spouse for a son or daughter
Autorickshaw	Small three-wheeled taxi
Ayah	Nanny servant
Bangers	English breakfast sausage
Beta	Affectionate term for boy, son
Beti	Affectionate term for girl, daughter
Bhagavad Gita	Most revered religious text for Hindus
Bhagwan	Refers to god or lord
Bindi	Decorative dot or sequin on the forehead for married woman
Brahmin	Highest caste
Chai	Tea cooked with milk
Chapati	Whole wheat flat bread cooked on a dry griddle
Chowkidar	Neighborhood night watchman
Coolie	Luggage porter at railroad station
Dal	Any cooked lentil
Dalit	Lowest caste
Dhaba	Informal roadside restaurant
Dhoti	Loose village pants
Firangi	A term used to refer to the British
Garara	For a bride, a fancy full skirt worn with a short top and veil
Gori	A very light-skinned female
Guru	Spiritual teacher
Ji	Term of respect added to a person's name

Glossary, *continued*

Joint Family	Newlyweds live with the groom's family
Kurta	Loose shirt
Lathi	Long bamboo pole carried by police and chowkidar
Mataji	Mother
Nan	Bread cooked in tandoor oven
Pajama	Men's two-piece cotton or silk lounging suit
Panchayat	Village judge and jury
Pani	Water
Pitaji	Father
Ram	God
Rupee	Indian currency, approximately 78 rupees to one dollar
Sabzi	Any cooked vegetable dish
Sadhu	A holy man, sage
Sari	Six to nine yards of cotton, silk, or synthetic fabric
Sherwani	Men's formal long coat
Shukria	Thank you
Tandoori	Any meat cooked on skewers in a tandoor oven

"India is the cradle of the human race, the birthplace of human speech, the mother of history, the grandmother of legend, and the great grandmother of tradition. Our most valuable and most instructive materials in the history of man are treasured up in India only."

Mark Twain

"I like the evening in India, the one magic moment when the sun balances on the rim of the world, and the hush descends, and ten thousand civil servants drift home on a river of bicycles, brooding on Lord Krishna and the cost of living."

James Cameron

Map of Northern India

Prologue

From my first visit with my husband Gopal in 1971, I've loved his home region of Punjab in Northern India with its flocks of green parrots arriving at sunset to sleep in the park's tallest trees, the Kashmiri shawl seller calling out specials from his bicycle cart, lines of freshly washed clothes snapping in the breeze, the papaya tree heavy with fruit, and tea and samosas with whoever dropped by in the afternoon full of funny stories to tell.

The pace of Indian life five decades ago was irresistible. Few people had phones or televisions, so visiting friends in the afternoon had developed into a high art, anticipated, unhurried and enjoyable.

Most importantly, when first arriving at the girls' orphanage in Patiala, I was struck by the children's smiles, good cheer, and gracious acceptance of their altered lives, lives with layers that seemed endless— tragedies and mysteries, superstitions and secrets, customs and rules that sometimes defied logic.

Six-year-old Preethi, beaten, then abandoned near the peanut vendor's stall and brought to the orphanage by passersby, Happy, an adorable two-year-old, discarded under a train seat for being female, Neena, who loved math and asked for workbooks instead of clothes or toys, sweet Sharan, who wanted to be a nurse and not be married off at seventeen, and beautiful Sushma, whose smile lit up every room she entered.

Jyoti, the eldest girl, whose parents were killed, saved her sister and made it to the orphanage, but loved a boy and defied the rigid rules. Smart, beautiful Nishu, whose mother poisoned her father and then ran off with her lover, came to the orphanage with her three younger sisters but later died, along with a sister, from juvenile diabetes because no one knew what to do. Some of these stories were inspired by the orphans and the countless working street children of Patiala and India, who had overcome so much in their short lives and understood the labyrinths they had to negotiate to make it out alive. I send you with my love, prayers, and belief in you always.

"[S]he went with him to India for the first time after they were married. Then it all made sense, and she realized that the hospitality he displayed to all guests was larger than he was – it was cultural, hereditary, something coded into his DNA."

Thrity Umrigar, The Story Hour

Love and Haight

Fresno, California

In 1964 I ordered a white with gold silk sari from a Hong Kong company but had no idea how it was worn. I needed an Indian woman, and my only source at the time was the local college's Foreign Student Advisor. She gave me seven names and phone numbers of male Indian students.

"They all know each other, one of them can help you," she said.

I dialed a number at random. A polite young man answered and seemed surprised by my interest in his country. After giving me the number of a female student, he said he would call in a few days and check if all went well. His name was Gopal Kapur.

Pammi, the Indian student, was most helpful in showing me how to wrap and tie the sari. A friend made the required short blouse and slip to complete the outfit. Gopal called a few days later, as promised.

Over the next six weeks, speaking only by phone, we discovered we liked foreign foods, travel, other cultures, and each other. When we finally met one Sunday in October, I opened the door to a slim young man dressed in a beautifully tailored double-breasted navy blazer with a raw silk tie. His gray wool slacks had creases sharp enough to cut cold butter. Over afternoon tea, he read poems to me in Urdu while I modeled the sari that had brought us together. My parents invited him to dinner, and he left at midnight. We were both intensely intrigued.

Gopal spent the next two years working as a civil engineer and then as an instructor of computer languages in San Francisco while I stayed in Fresno working at a bank. We met on weekends and holidays and planned to marry by February 1967, then one year away.

His parents ignored our registered letter to them in India asking for their blessing. A second letter with our appeal and now an April wedding date went unanswered.

Although we knew of Indian men who married non-Indians first and told their parents second, Gopal had traveled to Northern India six months earlier to plead our case in person. Any foreign daughter-in-law is met with suspicion and often open hostility.

However, not only was I divorced, I had a three-year-old daughter, thus rendering me beyond scandalous.

His planned six-week visit home stretched into a three-month detainment as his parents quickly got him professionally photographed, fitted for a new suit, and then hustled from home to home of numerous eligible women, hoping to get him quickly married and thereby render our relationship moot.

Almost as disturbing during his three-month absence, unbeknownst to either of us, a private detective was following me in Fresno. Desperate to find something that would convince Gopal I was not worthy, his parents, with the eager help of their nephew in Boston, hired the private eye to spy on me and send weekly reports.

I was unaware of the local and distant frenzy of activity and was preoccupied with the worry that Gopal had not, or could not, answer my letters, all sent to his friend's house in Patiala to thwart his father intercepting them. Finally, after over three weeks of no word, I used the one quick communication available and sent a telegram stating that if he didn't reply, "I'm coming." That got a telegraphed response that all was well and, "Letter to follow."

After Gopal finally returned to Fresno in late January, I learned he had been very ill in India. It took a doctor warning his parents that if they did not send him back to America, "I will not be responsible for the outcome" to goad them into reluctantly packing his bags. Tucked in his luggage were several letters from various bride prospects stating what they found "agreeable" about Gopal.

Two days after he returned, he found a business card wedged above his apartment doorknob with a note to call the printed number.

The detective answered and told Gopal that the agency had hired him to investigate me. He assumed I was some underworld moll or worse, knowing nothing of the story. Only after he realized I was harmless and my work and parenting routine exceedingly boring did he have a pang of conscience and decide to tell us. At that moment, I could have used the line; *I didn't know whether to laugh or cry.*

But in truth, I was angry. Early in Gopal's and my relationship, I had corresponded for several months with his father, exchanging pleasant letters about our two countries. However, once he realized that the young woman his son had suggested as a pen pal was now a possible daughter-in-law, the battle lines were drawn, and all was suddenly fair.

Gopal wanted his parents' blessings, as did I, but I was tired of the manipulation and devious behavior. In early April, a ray of hope appeared when we met with his parents' friend, Professor Razdan, who was in Los Angeles on a one-year teaching exchange. Gopal moved to San Francisco for work shortly after returning from India, so at the request of Gopal's parents, the professor flew up to San Francisco, and I drove from Fresno.

The meeting to look me over and report back took place during afternoon tea in the Garden Room of the Sheraton Palace Hotel. My inquisitor was not the typical middle-aged conservative Indian. He was, first and foremost, single and had an eye for the ladies. Handsome in an Omar Sharif meets Rossano Brazzi kind of way; he had gotten tuberculosis in his teens that left him with a damaged lung. This condition took him out of the prime Indian marriage market. It was a quirk of luck for us that after several months in free-wheeling--campus love is where you find it--Los Angeles, I, sitting there in a demure powder blue silk sari, pouring tea, looked positively border-line suitable.

We knew we had his approval after several "I don't know what all the fuss is about" type comments as he asked about my parents and our plans for the future.

Not surprisingly, even with the professor's endorsement, the letter with his parents' blessings remained elusive. We proceeded with a May date, unwilling to disrupt our lives further. I gave my notice at the bank and began packing for our wedding and my daughter's and my move to San Francisco.

On the periphery of our consciousness was the parallel world of the hippy revolution swirling around us in San Francisco. It didn't interest us beyond the usual comments on their outlandish dress, drowsy drug behavior, and open-armed philosophies. Compared to what we were going through, they seemed silly and self-indulgent. But their music, lifestyle, and The Haight, as San Franciscans referred to Haight Ashbury, were getting major press and global attention.

Every weekend, I drove my stick shift VW Bug up and down the city's hills, looking at apartments and sites for our wedding luncheon. Traffic jams had to be circumvented as out-of-towners poured in with wide-eyed relatives from the mid-west in search of the "peace" crowd. Drivers yelled to the first people they could find, "Where're the hippies?" Locals would point west, and cars would zoom off, confident their quarry would be on the next corner.

A new Jamaican restaurant had received rave reviews, so we drove to the address, only to find the place was one block from the now famous intersection of Height and Ashbury. Police officers stood on corners while mounted traffic cops tried to control gridlock as thousands of cars crawled along Haight and passengers ogled the scene. They were not disappointed.

Impulse-driven and drug-choreographed dancers would twirl and bounce to bongo drums as young women took off their clothes and threw flowers at the police. Our little Bug was almost lost in the melee. Unable to go forward or backward, we could only shrug helplessly when a cop slapped the hood of our car and told us to move.

Mothers with baby strollers were being pushed into the street by excited weekend hippies. These were young, white-collar professionals who rented long wigs and beards, wore raggedy pants with tie-dyed shirts and flooded the Haight, eager for the Age of Aquarius on their days off. They sang louder, smoked harder, and danced longer. A show in itself was watching resident hippies amble up behind the interlopers, pull off their wigs, and then offer them a toke.

Our wedding took place on May 6, 1967, in the home of Dr. Chaudhary, a thoughtful, gentle man who had authored five books on comparative religion and had a popular inter-faith church across from Golden Gate Park's Panhandle. As we stood on the Chaudhary's front steps, smiling for home movies and photos, we were unaware that this immediate neighborhood would become nationally and internationally famous. We were married in the corner house of 25th and Castro, now, years later, the heart of the Castro District.

Gopal wore a pink silk and gold *sherwani*, the formal coat his grandfather had worn to the court of the then Maharaja of Patiala, and a gold turban borrowed from an Indian friend in San Francisco. I wore one of the only three silk saris I had. An iridescent green, though wedding colors are usually red or bright pink for women.

One of Gopal's students, Jimmy, a florist friend, made our garlands and did the bird of paradise and blue iris arrangements for our wedding. At our Indian luncheon, he was seated next to John Andrews, the head of Merrill Lynch in Fresno, whose wife, Carol, had worked at the American Consulate in

Bombay. A Hindu friend from the Fiji Islands gave a humorous toast, and later, Gopal's older, southern bell secretary, Irene, helped us carry our gifts to the car before our Persian friend, Masood, drove us to the airport. To complete this picture of ecumenical serendipity, we honeymooned at Disneyland.

The letter of acceptance came with Draconian timing a week after our wedding.

Leaving our wedding reception, San Francisco, May 1967

"India lives in several centuries at the same time."

Arundhati Roy

Two Loves, One Pledge

July 1971: Patiala, Northern India

It had been four years since our wedding in California, and we were in India for me to meet my in-laws for the first time. The tension over our marriage calmed in September of 1968 with the birth of our son, Raj, the first grandchild. Landing on April second in New Delhi and then on to Patiala, 160 miles north, these past three months had been the hottest days and nights our children and I had ever experienced. The swamp cooler in our bedroom window lived up to its name. Water circulating through straw pads that surrounded the fan created even more humidity. A leather purse grew surface mold in the damp, heavy air. Nightly blackouts stopped all the fans; only the mega-wealthy homes had air conditioning.

I was the one American for miles around and became free entertainment for the neighborhood. When Gopal and I took a simple evening walk around the block, little boys would trail after us, fascinated with the *gori*. Children would see us coming and run to alert the household.

My mother-in-law had the final word on what I wore when I left the house. Since I was new and meeting relatives and family friends for the first time, I could not greet visitors without dressing up. Only a new silk sari, fresh flowers in my hair, full makeup, and a complete set of gold jewelry would do—embarrassing my in-laws by skipping any of these essentials was out of the question.

I wrote to a friend in California: "Imagine sitting in a sauna set on high, dressed in a tight silk blouse, wrapped snugly in a silk sheet, with a bicycle chain around your neck...almost daily, for weeks."

I wasn't the only person adjusting to a new situation. My sweet mother-in-law was a strict religious vegetarian. She must have been aghast when three beef eaters moved in. Gopal was also non-veg by now but returned effortlessly to a meatless diet for his mom as soon as we landed in Delhi. I had no trouble giving up meat, but our daughter, Jennifer, eight, and son, Raj, almost three, needed protein.

Then Gopal's mother made a dispensation. She announced she would cook eggs, only for the grandchildren, in a special pan to be washed outside by one of us. Though Gopal explained to her the eggs were not fertile, it was a lifetime of observance never to eat a dead animal, up against a minute of logic--we lost. If Gopal occasionally wanted eggs, we waited until she left for the market, did a quick scramble, washed the egg pan with soap and the garden hose, and put it away.

It was early July and our last night in Patiala. Tomorrow we're moving to the capital. Gopal's first book on *IBM Assembler Language Programming* caused a stir in the programming world, and he's been offered a position with IBM in Delhi. We'll be staying as paying guests with a non-veg Sikh family. The room includes a full bathroom, a house phone, and a window air conditioner. Though my in-laws, hoping for a semblance of a joint family, were sorely disappointed. Gopal started with IBM four weeks previously, leaving the children and me in Patiala six hours away until we could find housing in Delhi.

My father-in-law, a college president several hours north, came home only on weekends. Mataji did not speak English. We communicated with my few words of Punjabi, hand gestures, nods, and shrugs. There was no telephone or television; the only English radio was BBC, which came and went between static storms. No English newspapers and no car.

Having read my three paperbacks from home twice, I was reading labels off the kitchen supplies when a neighbor loaned me her *Femina* magazine collection. Printed in English, *Femina* was a cross between *Good Housekeeping* and *People*—circa India in the 1970s. Only fashion, recipes, and Bollywood news, but I was desperate. I soon learned who the current stars were and the titles of the top movies. This, more than anything, surprised my in-laws' friends.

When visitors came for tea, the conversation was in Hindi or Punjabi. Our children and I were expected to sit for hours, dressed to the nines, smiling pleasantly while the room pointed, stared, and discussed us head to toe.

Occasionally, someone would address me in English, and my mother-in-law would become anxious if I laughed out loud or tried to join in a 'mixed' conversation with men.

Jennifer and Raj had a generous supply of neighborhood children eager to play. But I was suffocating in the unrelenting humid heat and the isolation from all things familiar. On some days, when the only activity was a dairy farmer herding a few water buffalo down the lane, I felt I'd been teleported to the sixteenth century. Worse was the knowledge, idling just out of consciousness, that if one of our children should become seriously ill, we were three hours from a semi-modern hospital and competent doctors, providing we could find a car and driver.

One morning, while Gopal was in Delhi, Jennifer woke with thick, red, ropy welts all over her face, ears, and neck. She had no known allergies, so my first thought was a severe bite. Jen's face was alarming, so Mataji sent the gardener's son to fetch the nearest family doctor six blocks away. An hour went by, then three, then four. I was frantic. Jen finally mustered a look in the mirror and started crying. As we waited into the eighth hour, I put useless cold clothes on her face to comfort her that something was being done. By the time the doctor arrived, the welts had subsided somewhat, and he acted as though we had wasted his valuable time. He had no explanation for the condition, and it disappeared by the next day.

Accustomed to the freedom to solve my problems or hop in a car to get things done, I was stifled at every turn.

Then, I had an ever-so-minor meltdown about not being able to lock our bedroom door at night. The first morning in Patiala, my in-laws burst into our bedroom at 7 a.m. It sounded like a police raid. Interior doors are heavy, affixed on both sides with thick slide bolts at the top, middle, and bottom that rattle and bang when the double doors hit the walls. Our children, sleeping in the same room, were terrified---and all for a cup of hand-delivered "bed tea." Though brought as a sincere welcome, it was the first of many cultural misunderstandings.

On this one issue, I put my foot down. There is little regard, or concept, for personal privacy (most heads of households open everyone's mail), but I was adamant. We locked the door at night and added fresh fodder for discussion with visitors at afternoon tea.

Despite the heat, the cultural canyons, and the people's astonishing tolerance for everyday inconvenience, I loved the differentness of India. From the moment our plane's doors swung open at 4 a.m., and I first breathed in the unique smoky smell of all that she is, I felt a kinship and completeness. India is a beloved older sister, secure in my devotion, allowing me to complain and criticize occasionally. I know she will absorb and understand my little difficulties and welcome me back, again and again.

India's children are beautiful inside and out, with respectfulness and gentleness that western children would do well to emulate. I loved the refreshing absence of daily griping about personal woes or life in general. India withstood Alexander the Great, the Moguls, and the British. Now she smiles patiently at my little dust devils and suggests a cup of tea.

So, with Gopal back for the move, all that last day, I happily packed for the six-hour drive to Delhi the following morning. The only obligation left was to attend a dinner that evening at the home of the local communist chief.

India has always had an odd tolerance for the Communist Party. They controlled several states, and at one time, Russia had finagled and wheedled to place a communist agent openly in almost every city of democratic India. It was common to see a Russian calendar hanging in village homes, with Kodakquality photos of Russian-built dams and power plants in India. Though the Iron Curtain would start to lift the following year, with Nixon's visit to Moscow—Americans considered Communist Russia enemy number one.

This local Indian Communist had a seventeen-year-old daughter who had failed her university entrance exams. Thinking he would finesse my father-in-law into applying his influence and getting her admitted against the rules, he set out to woo him with every trick in his opportunistic book, including transportation to dinner.

Since we were leaving the next morning, I was in an upbeat mood. After sending a car and driver to ferry us to his home, which reminded me of a one-story Spanish hacienda, he ushered us into his living room. His wife was waiting and namasted and bowed to each of us--major apple polishing had commenced.

There was also a western-looking man and woman seated to one side. Before meeting them, I caught Gopal's eye and glanced down at the coffee table. Spread across the surface was every book in the Time-Life series. Most of the Disney characters were on a lower shelf, in 6-inch high plastic, with Mickey Mouse in the center. Our communist, eager to impress, was displaying some of his most prized possessions—very difficult to get in India in the 70s. When we met his other guests, it screamed volumes about the capriciousness of regional Indian politics.

I assumed they were a married couple, especially when a blonde girl, Jennifer's age, came down the hall and stood shyly next to the woman. Au contraire. With a servile bend to his back, our host introduced the man as Russia's chief agent for Punjab State and the woman, with daughter in tow, as his handler ("Esteemed comrade") from Moscow. After we shook hands, our hostess herded the ladies to one end of the long room anchored by a leather L-shaped couch. The men retired to the room's opposite end, where Johnny Walker Black Label was generously served around my teetotaler father-in-law.

I ended up next to enemy # 1, who spoke British accented English, and bristled with; *we have more guided missiles than you do,* hostility. As I handed her a Time-Life book on, *The American Revolution,* she asked me why I was wearing Indian clothes. "Out of respect for my husband's parents and because I want to," I answered. She sniffed and looked wistfully at the men drinking. Our hostess was busy directing the servant girl in passing out trays of hot snacks from the kitchen.

Jennifer walked to the handler's daughter and, in child-speak, invited her to play on the shaded patio near where we sat. Someone produced a jump rope, and with our son watching from a porch swing, they quickly became oblivious to the currents in the room.

My father-in-law, forced to use English with the Russian agent, was expounding on the delights of democracy with his usual declarative statements. I smothered a grin and passed my enemy the potato rounds fried in spicy garbanzo batter with mint sauce.

Before being called to the dinner table, where all stops had been pulled, the Russian mother and probable KGB agent asked me triumphantly, "Why is it that over twenty percent of you Americans are in mental hospitals?"

Patriotism suddenly leaped, bright-eyed, to my sleeve, activating DefCon5. I was the only homegrown American in the room, and she was a homegrown communist bully. Gopal would have matched her with stealth and logic, but he was busy with a face-off of his own across the room, judging from the proud chortles coming from Pitaji. I parried with how badly misled she was.

"Had you the freedom we have to research propaganda, you would know how ridiculous that statistic is." She harrumphed and looked again at the men drinking.

I said, "It's deplorable, don't you agree, that there are so many alcoholics in your country? I believe the World Health Organization put the recent figure at over sixteen percent."

I remembered vaguely reading something along those lines, but all is fair in war, even this proton-sized one.

My mother-in-law, ever mindful of my speaking out, noted the change in my tone and began wringing her hands. Still holding *The American Revolution* in her lap, the handler opened her mouth to counter punch, but at that moment, our Indian host, regretting, I'm sure, that he didn't have trumpets, grandly summoned us to dinner. The children came in laughing and holding hands, adding just the right note of ironic absurdity to the scene.

The dinner, and evening, ended with a polite whimper and all for naught. My father-in-law did nothing to help the daughter of our hosts, and she ended up attending a mediocre college in Russia.

The following day, we stuffed the bags and ourselves into a small Indian Ambassador sedan. Like most in India, our driver had never heard of a driving test, thus ensuring our lives would flash before our eyes numerous times before we reached Delhi.

Ambassadors did not have air conditioning in the seventies and scant insulation. The monsoons were late, causing the rust-colored dust to hang in the moist air for hours. We were coated with a gritty tan as it seeped and blew into everything. When we got to Delhi, windows down all the way, we were hot, tired, and dirty.

Our car was winding its way through the heart of the city when Gopal remarked that we were nearing Embassy Row. I had been cut off from news of home for months, thinking only of a cool shower and a newspaper, when I looked up.

As we came around a long, soft curve lined with stately trees, a flash of red appeared between the leaves for an instant. I straightened up. The canopy was dense, but a second later, the trees parted, and like arms opening to embrace us, there was our flag, our beautiful Stars and Stripes, a piece of home welcoming us back into the fold.

Gopal told the driver to stop the car. We got out, covered in dirt, and stood drinking in the white marble embassy, our handsome Marines standing guard and Old Glory waving majestically in the afternoon breeze. If a marching band had appeared playing "God Bless America," I wouldn't have been surprised. We put our hands to our hearts, and with white lines tracking down our dusty cheeks, my family and I recited the pledge of allegiance. It was the 4th of July 1971.

We were in India for five more months and had a wonderful experience living in cosmopolitan Delhi. By our next trip, four years later, India's honeymoon with Russia was over, though the party remained a presence in Parliament.

That December, three days after we left for home, India and Pakistan's hostilities grew to the brink of war, and the Delhi airport was closed for weeks. Sixty-five miles north of Patiala, in Amritsar, a civilian became a national hero after shooting down three Pakistani warplanes with a machine gun mounted on the roof of his home. He was a Muslim.

The sight of our flag flying over the American Embassy in any foreign country never fails to put a lump in my throat.

With Gopal and my father-in-law, in center.
All is forgiven.

With my mother-in-law in her garden

"There are some parts of the world that, once visited, get into your heart and won't go. For me, India is such a place. When I first visited, I was stunned by the richness of the land, by its lush beauty and exotic architecture, by its ability to overload the senses with the pure, concentrated intensity of its colors, smells, tastes, and sounds. It was as if all my life I had been seeing the world in black and white and, when brought face-to-face with India, experienced everything re-rendered in brilliant technicolor."

Keith Bellows

Driving to India

Patiala, India: 1971

I'm dressing after my second bucket bath since morning--the only quick relief to an Indian summer in high humid gear. My mother-in-law knocks on the thick wooden door. In her limited English, she announces, "Mrs. America here, you."

As I hurry to tie my sari, muted voices come through, and I'm surprised to hear a woman speaking American English. After three months in India, a visitor from home would be a treat. In the living room, I find a strawberry blonde (Julie Christie mixed with Sissy Spacek) in her late twenties, sitting on the couch talking with my husband, Gopal.

My mother-in-law hovers nearby, unsure what to do with another American woman. Gopal asks for lemonade just as the electricity comes back after a morning blackout, and ceiling fans stir the air.

In the early 70s, there were maybe, six Americans in all of Patiala, then the size of Berkeley. Two were male missionaries, one with a wife, and three were wives of Indian husbands.

Sharon introduces herself as the woman behind the wheel of the blue Dodge sedan seen around the bazaar. American cars in India are rare. The expense of shipping them from the States is exorbitant, and finding competent mechanics is almost impossible outside New Delhi and the big port cities.

Sharon tells us she's married to a Sikh, and they're staying with his family for the summer. We exchange adjusting to India stories. She can't believe her father-in-law opens her mail and looks through her suitcases with impunity, and I can't understand a country that produces millions of engineers hasn't thought to put handles on cooking pots. We visit over lemonade and peanuts for a while, and then I ask about the car.

In the spring of 1971, she and her husband, Jitender (Jit) Singh, 6'2", with a full beard and turban, retire from their jobs at IBM in New York City, cash in half of their shares of Big Blue, store their possessions and go shopping for a car. The quickest way to India from the U.S. is by air. Sharon and Jit decide to drive.

They settle on a showroom new four-door Dodge. The couple's families and friends see them off as they drive to the New Jersey docks, where they ship the car to a port in Oslo, Norway. While waiting to claim their car in Europe, they study maps and plot their route to India. Neither Jit nor Sharon speaks a European language fluently, and this will be Sharon's first trip outside the United States.

The only timetable is getting to India by July for a relative's wedding, so after claiming their car, they decide to drive north from Oslo and see Sweden. Then, taking a giant hairpin turn, they come south again through Finland. The maps don't show the fjords or that the only road in '71 snakes along 400-foot-high cliffs for miles with no guard rails. Blind turns are common; rock slides halt the sparse traffic for hours while drivers remove the rocks and rubble themselves. Sharon says this drive, in some ways, was the most frightening time of their entire trip. But so much more was to come.

Finally reaching the southernmost point of Finland, they take an auto ferry from Helsinki to Tallinn, Estonia, and begin the first leg of their journey through Eastern Europe.

At the Polish border, Sharon tells us Jit's turban, his American wife, and their new car are suspect. The Poles have never seen anyone driving to India; it is unthinkable. To lighten the mood, Sharon asks an English-speaking guard if he has ever been to India. He frowns and says he has no reason to leave Poland. They are finally allowed to enter after Jit shows them their wedding photos, the port receipt for their car, and visas for India.

After passing through Hungary, they decide to spend two days in Bucharest, Romania. Everything is going well until one of the Romanian border guards asks (with gestures and grunts) for a lift to the next town.

It's soon apparent the man is drunk and smitten with their car. Sitting in the back seat with his rifle slung casually over his shoulder, he sings while caressing the upholstery and clicking the ceiling light on and off with child-like fascination.

When they reach the small town, the man directs them to his house, where Jit and Sharon must take the man's parents, then his wife and children, and finally the neighbors for rides, honking the horn continually at everyone's gleeful insistence.

Their host pulls them to the house for drinks and food, but a crowd has gathered around the Dodge, and Jit is worried about the car remaining in one piece. They somehow escape without offending their gun-toting host and get to Bucharest around midnight.

Their trip philosophy; travel light, buy what they need along the way, and look for shelter when they get to their next stop. Reservations mean structure and schedules; after their high-stress jobs, that's the last thing they want. But, it also means, at times, there's no room at the inn, hostel, or even a no-star hotel.

The first night in Bucharest is spent near the car, in sleeping bags, in a city park. They wake to find a large family of gypsies sitting around them in a circle. The gypsies had never seen such a big car, and Jit fascinates them. He's wrapping his turban and smoothing his beard when one of the older women hisses, "He's a jinni!" This comment is translated for Jit by a university student observing the curious scene. He later helps them rescue their car from a crowd of young men.

The gypsy women insist Jit read their palms. The body posturing says it all: Jit is one of them, and Sharon is an interloper who should get lost. The atmosphere gets tense until Jit has an idea. Sitting on a rug their prettiest young woman has rolled out for him, Jit reads a palm and then calls Sharon over to confirm his reading. The women are confused; what does she know—a blonde foreigner in Bermuda shorts?

Whispering in English and conferring in Hindi (Greek to Sharon), they nod, frown, and then have an enlightened vision of something they can mime. A baby in arms from Sharon, riches or a new love from Jit--all good fortunes, and the gypsies finally roll up their rug, cast a last, wistful look at Jit, and leave satisfied.

Their *European Hostel Directory* shows that a Bucharest Hostel family room guarantees privacy with a shower for five dollars a night. One becomes available, and they gratefully rest, write letters, do laundry, and enjoy local wine with hot meals for two days.

Turkey, resembling a big potato on the latitudes, is the next border on their due east course. A cousin of Jit's at the Indian Embassy in Ankara invites them to stay a couple of days. They'll make calls home to New York and get their car serviced before their next big leg—through Iran, hilly Afghanistan, and Pakistan.

Cousin Rakesh (Rocky) takes the day off and shows Jit and Sharon around Ankara, where Sharon attracts a few hard stares. At first, she refuses to wear a scarf, long sleeves, and slacks. It's now summer and hot, but Rocky insists. Combing a nearby bazaar, they find a suitable gauzy shirt and scarf that lets in some air. That night, as they leave a restaurant and walk to the car, Jit gets a bad feeling.

"Didn't we park right here by this tobacco shop?" Rocky surveys the street, nodding. The Dodge is gone, and Jit is guilt-ridden. *Did I lock the door, or were we talking, and I forgot?*

Sharon's stomach drops. Rocky had hired one of the countless street children to watch the car, a standard practice that allows the child to earn some money rather than be labeled a beggar.

The three set out to find little Ali, who said he lived around the corner. All they see is an empty lot about twenty-five feet wide. A small lean-to with a red glow coming through uneven wooden slats sits at the back. Rocky calls out for Ali, but a bigger boy emerges from the gloom carrying an iron bar. "Who wants him?"

Rocky knows he cannot appear frightened or hesitant.

"We hired Ali to watch our car tonight, and the car is missing. The police are on their way."

The older boy seems to relax and even appears sheepish in the shadows. "Well then, you have no problem because they took your car."

Little Ali comes out at that moment and apologizes. He's a businessman himself, he explains, and with that, he hands back the three Turkish bills Rocky had paid him earlier.

Hearing "police," Jit asks, "What's going on?"

Rocky tells Jit and Sharon to follow him as he trots quickly from the lot to the main street and flags down a taxi.

"I've got to make a call. What time is it?"

Sharon looks at her luminous dial, "Midnight."

"Such is life. He'll be angry, but he owes me one."

"Who'll be angry? What's happening, Rocky?"

"Look, cousin, sometimes, on a slow day, the police pick up foreign cars on bogus charges and hold them until money is paid. I've got to call Mr. Patel, the undersecretary, to the ambassador. He owes me a big favor." Rocky tells the driver to take them to the Intercontinental Hotel—one of the few places with public phones open all night.

Patel says he will meet them at the police station in one hour. Sharon is relieved but anxious; if the car's been stripped or damaged, the delay could cost them. They had plans to get the Dodge checked out by a mechanic working for the American Embassy, another Rocky connection. The junior functionary has been busy somehow racking up credits. Jit is curious but doesn't ask—rescuing the car is all-important.

After an hour of bluster and bluff, the senior police officer on duty backs off and returns the car with only a non-negotiable $25 fine for being three inches too close to a corner. Since they had parked in the middle of the block, this was when Sharon told us, "I knew I wasn't anywhere west of the Atlantic."

Three hours before sunrise, Rocky drops them at his flat and parks the car in the embassy lot for safekeeping. They are relieved to find the Dodge undamaged except for a few scratches from the tow chain.

Two days later, with fresh supplies of film, small gifts for helpers along the way, food, another medical kit, three gallons of drinking water, and two gallons for the radiator, they hug Rocky and thank him for his invaluable help. As Jit opens his door to get in, Rocky pulls him aside.

"Look, I've talked to people at work, and we all agree you should take this for Afghanistan and Pakistan." Jit looks down as Rocky opens an ordinary brown paper sack, and inside are a large handgun and two boxes of ammunition.

"Whoa! You're crazy; we can't take this."

"Yes, you must, Jit. Listen, Afghanistan has road pirates and local feudal lords who set up 'toll' barriers. They'll take one look at Sharon and...."

Sobered, Jit says, "Rocky, I've never fired a gun in my life."

"You won blue ribbons in archery, didn't you?"

"Yes, but..."

"You have a good eye and steady hands. Follow me; it will only be a little delay." And before they can argue, Rocky jumps in his jeep and tears off down the street, with Jit and Sharon following in bewilderment.

Jit learns his gun is a Colt 45, made for the U.S. Navy, with a six-shot capacity. With the help of an Indian Army instructor attached to the embassy, Jit has a steady hand and a good eye. Sharon also has a respectable hit pattern on her paper target. With a list of gun do's and don'ts, they say a second goodbye and promise to call Rocky as soon as they get to India. The look of concern on Rocky's face will return to haunt Jit.

Crossing Turkey takes all day, but by late afternoon in the distance, they can see their goal: the city of Van. Zabel, an Armenian friend from IBM, has arranged for Jit and Sharon to stay with her aunt and uncle in Van for one night. Exhausted and not knowing what to expect, Jit and Sharon are relieved to be met at the door by a delightful and erudite couple.

Aunty and Uncle Mardekian invite two English-speaking couples for cocktails, who regale Jit and Sharon with funny stories. Jit has them laughing over his gypsy meeting and soon has to read the ladies' palms after intense teasing, good-natured begging, and the rolling out of a small Turkish rug.

In the morning, Sharon wakes to view Van Lake, the largest in Turkey. The Mardekian's roomy flat is smartly appointed with modern furnishings and beautiful regional rugs. After presenting their hosts with gifts from their niece in New York, Sharon and Jit give the couple a bottle of Kentucky's finest bourbon (a hint from Zabel) and a book of American poems. Jit suggests a ride in the Dodge, and Uncle directs them along the lake's marina, where the car draws curious looks and unabashed waves from admirers.

After convincing Jit and Sharon to stay one more night and rest up for Iran, they stop for lunch, and Sharon falls in love with Armenian food. Aunty Mardekian is delighted. "You must try lamajoon, sarma, and suborag, though I make it better at home," she adds with a wink. Thin, crusty mini pizzas made with a spicy tomato and ground lamb topping, grape leaves stuffed with rice, ground lamb, and pine nuts, and a flaky, triangular pastry filled with cheese and chopped parsley fill their plates. Tall, cold glasses of taan, thinned yogurt whipped with a bit of salt, and grated cucumber, are brought by a jovial waiter.

Uncle Mardekian follows his meal with a cigar, and a cup of Turkish coffee, threatening to ask Jit to "read" the grounds - an Armenian and Turkish custom - if he doesn't join him with a cigar.

The following day, with maps and cautions about Iran from Uncle, who lived in Tabriz for a few years, Jit and Sharon say a reluctant goodbye to the warm, hospitable couple and head for the Iranian border. With heavy Western investment and influence during the '70s, getting across Iran on good highways was relatively easy. After one night in Tehran, they fill the tank, adding a full two-liter gas can in the trunk, and, leaving at dawn, make it to the Afghanistan border by late afternoon.

Following Rocky's advice, they pull over and tuck the gun into a small pocket of space the mechanic had made (at Rocky's insistence) inside the front left fender. To reach the weapon, a searcher must lift the hood and run his hand alongside hot engine parts. Sharon puts her long-sleeved shirt and scarf back on, but nothing can disguise the fact she is foreign and blonde.

Jit left India when he was fourteen and has visited just once since. He is slightly more informed about the following two countries than Sharon. He knows the Muslim culture a little, but there are regional differences, with enough taboos, superstitions, and biases to keep a team of scholars (or sociologists) busy over a lifetime. Muslim men find foreign women fascinating, yet consider them almost prostitutes unless they are with their husbands or a male relative.

All Iran-Afghanistan border checkpoints are busy, with lines of cars, scooters, and trucks backed up for half a mile. The dusty Dodge is about fiftieth in line when a young American man runs up to the car and says he is with the U.S. Embassy and can get them through on his pass if they give him a lift.

Michael Porter explains he hitch-hikes every weekend. "My girlfriend is with the Peace Corps in Herat." With Michael's diplomatic pass, the three are bumped to the head of the line. That night, Sharon and Jit stay with the corps project director and his wife. Before departing at sunrise, they meet a group of Canadians and Americans digging wells for nearby villages.

The Dodge's front right tire blows in high foothills, forty miles east of Herat. There's no other traffic in sight, but Sharon is uneasy as they quickly unload the trunk and bring out the spare. While Jit struggles with the jack on the uphill ground, Sharon retrieves and loads the gun before tucking it in her pocket.

The tire is finally on, and they are reloading the trunk when they hear jingly bells. Around a curve, two giant camels appear loaded with bedding and clanging pots and pans. Three little heads pop up out of the baggage rolls and stare at the strange vehicle and the woman standing alongside it.

Behind the camels, two rough, turbaned men with rifles slung across their backs ride on horseback. Seeing Sharon, they jerk their horses to a halt and call the camels to stop. Jit is bent over, repacking a bag, and momentarily out of sight.

Everyone stares for several moments before the two men dismount and swing their rifles forward. What had looked like bedding moves, and two cloth-covered shapes take form on the camels, pulling the children to them. The men mutter and begin approaching the car just as Jit stands up from behind the trunk. He calls out a standard Urdu greeting, "*Salaam Alaikum*," and the transformation is instant.

The men halt, nod, and return the greeting as their eyes switch back and forth between the two *firangis*. Sharon keeps her grip on the gun and pulls her scarf lower over her face. One of the men asks something, and Jit replies, "*Hindustan*," the Middle Eastern term for India. This seems to satisfy their curiosity, and they remount their horses, trotting off down the road behind the swaying camels without a backward glance.

Shaken by the encounter, the realization washes over the couple that they've been naïve about their safety. Their pistol will stop some attackers up close, but they are helpless against long guns. Passing through small villages, they notice a rifle is slung across the back of every man not doing a task, and the culture is primitive. There are no telephone poles for miles, and only the occasional scooter is parked at a dwelling. Wood fires keep a smoky haze in the air throughout the day. They attract attention as children run after their car, yelling and waving frantically — several times, young men on horseback gallop alongside, staring at Sharon.

Jit hopes to reach Kabul, another 300 miles east, by dark, but the hilly road is scarred with potholes and deep ruts. Forty miles per hour is their top speed, only in short spurts. They eat without stopping and press on, anxious to find modern services before dark.

Shortly before sunset, they finally come to a dusty town at the base of the foothills. Sharon sees something that lifts her spirits as they search for a gas pump. "It was like coming out of a black, foggy sea and spying a lighthouse. We were elated."

Plunked down in the 16th-century setting is a small brick Catholic Church. After locking the car, they push and pull on a weathered handle, but the church door won't budge. Walking around to the side through a creaking iron gate, they find an elderly priest picking pomegranates from a grove of six old trees. He's Irish and delighted to meet them. Father Thomas invites them to a dinner of goat and potato stew cooked with pomegranate juice ("It tenderizes the meat," he explains), flat roti bread, and rice. Later, sitting in the garden with cups of tea and dates around a kerosene lantern, they tell him about their travels.

"You've bitten off quite a chew," he says after listening quietly. "The educated Afghan is one of the most hospitable, warm, and loyal people I've had the blessing to know. But, except for acquiring guns, the tribal people have not changed much in the past 200 years. They disdain education, carry grudges over generations, and are hostile to strangers. Pakistani villagers are just as dangerous; you really must be careful."

Father Thomas puts them up for the night in a tiny room next to the church kitchen. The next morning, he gives them a sack of pomegranates and insists on sending Harry, the fourteen-year-old son of the Afghan Christian gardener, to Kabul with them, two hours east.

"He's done this before; he'll hitch a ride back, and it gets him out from under his father's thumb for a day." Before leaving Father Thomas, Sharon and Jit put a generous offering in the church box and thanked this kind and gentle man for his hospitality.

Harry is a delight. He speaks heavily accented English and entertains them with his dreams of becoming a movie star, "Like Cleent Eesvood and Bort Reenals!" Shortly before reaching Kabul, the red engine light comes on. Jit pulls over, and Harry immediately begins directing traffic around their car, standing with the authority of a police chief and swinging an "official" arm when traffic gets too close.

After some time, they decide it's only a faulty light. Buoyed by the news, Harry talks them into a movie starring his hero, whom he praises all the way to the city. The Kabul Theater is surprisingly plush, with red velvet ropes around cushy VIP seats. Vendors come down the aisles selling hot roasted peanuts and warm bottles of cola. As the audience cheers and stamps their feet whenever "Cleent" defeats a villain, Harry raises one eyebrow and nods knowingly.

A roadside dinner of lamb kabobs, rice, and watermelon fortifies them as Harry shows Jit the crossroads where he will catch a ride home. Sharon tucks fifty Afghani bills into the boy's pocket, but he pulls them out and hands them back, offended.

Deeply aggrieved, with his right hand over his heart, he whispers, "You are my Aunty."

Sharon tries to explain, "We want you safe, Harry." Jit doesn't want a truck driver demanding something from this innocent boy in exchange for a ride. Harry picks up the thread of their concern and produces a long, curved dagger from under his loose shirt. "Safe I'm traveling, Uncle," he assures Jit, man to man. They wait in the Dodge nearby until Harry is picked up about an hour later.

"It was silly, I suppose, but I wanted the driver to see Harry waving goodbye and realize that someone cares for this boy," Sharon tells us.

After a welcomed night's sleep at a decent inn recommended by Father Thomas, and a breakfast of boiled eggs, fruit, and bread, they check the oil and tires, refuel, and feel the tingle of anticipation. India is just 600 miles east.

At the last moment, before leaving Kabul, Sharon decides to run into the American Embassy to see if she can call home. Jit stays outside with the fully-loaded car. She finishes the call and then takes several letters to the front desk to mail. Seeing the Dodge through the window, the clerk asks about the car, and Sharon tells him about their trip and destination. He looks at her letters and asks if her last name is Singh.

"Yes, why?"

"Is your husband Indian by birth?" he continues, ignoring her question.

"Yes, why do you ask?"

"You must know he won't be allowed to cross into Pakistan since the two countries are talking all-out war."

"He's an American citizen with an American passport; they won't stop him."

"I strongly recommend he checks with the Indian Embassy before you attempt to cross. Their building is one street over."

Jit sees Sharon hesitating on the steps. Thinking she's gotten bad news from home, he rushes to her.

"Jit, it may be nothing, but the embassy clerk says you won't be allowed to cross into Pakistan, and we've got to double-check at the Indian Embassy." As they hurry, Sharon explains the talk of war.

"I'm an American," Jit protests. *But you look like an Indian Sikh, and no one will stop to ask before they shoot,* Sharon answers in her thoughts.

The Indian staffer is painfully polite while assuring them it would be a bad idea to attempt entry into Pakistan.

"Feelings are most tense these days, Mr. Singh. The Paki's will stop whomever they deem a spy or a threat."

Sharon and Jit are rattled. How did they miss the situation? Rocky would have told them—but would they have listened?

The irony is that until 1947, what is now Pakistan was part of India. In 1971, there were still millions of Muslim Pakistanis who had been born and raised in India, with affectionate feelings towards Hindu Indians—old neighbors and friends. The hostilities remain political and between governments, centering on Kashmir. Jit's father was born in what is now Lahore, Pakistan. He refuses to believe the border officials won't let him through on his American passport, which carried considerable weight in the seventies.

With half the morning gone, they hurry to Torkham, the nearest Afghani border town. No one thinks to check with the Pakistani Embassy in Kabul. They reach Torkham early afternoon and decide Jit should first attempt to cross on foot, but he is refused entry. As he's leaving, he observes a shift change. "Let's come back and try again with the new crew."

After refueling and a quick roadside meal, they drive up to the guards as a small Pakistani Army convoy pulls up behind them. Seeing Jit, the guards, aware of the soldiers watching, are steely-eyed and suspicious. One official hints at a bribe, but Jit wants in cleanly.

Sharon backs the car up and parks nearby as the first prickles of desperation take hold. At that moment, a smartly dressed Pakistani Army officer wearing a black beret at a rakish angle strolls to their car. In impeccable Oxford English, Major Khan tells them Sharon can follow the convoy to Lahore, and they will keep an eye on her, but, "Sorry, old boy." Jit will not be allowed across.

They have minutes to decide as they watch the soldiers taking a break. They can return to Kabul, abandon the car and fly over their problem, or Sharon can drive across Pakistan alone, and Jit will fly to India, meeting her at the border. He is in agony. For over ten weeks, their car has been their American home away from home, a trusted piece of the familiar where ever they are. Sharon grips the steering wheel.

"I'm not giving up this car, Jit, not after all we've been through. She won't fail me. I can do this. I know it." They look into each other's eyes, saying a thousand things. Then, as they watch the soldiers putting out their cigarettes, it is decided. Jit will take a taxi back to Kabul and fly to Delhi, then to Amritsar, a city with the nearest airport to Wagah, the Pakistani border crossing to India. With no way to communicate, their fates will be unknown until they reunite at the border. They estimate the worst and best driving times Sharon can expect with a quick overnight in Lahore. Jit throws a few things into a duffle bag, and they hug goodbye. The last thing he does is double-check the gun.

Sharon shoves it in her bag under her seat and pulls up behind the last army truck. Jit is quickly lost in the dust clouds stirred by the milling crowds and honking traffic behind her. Cars, trucks, bullock carts, bicycles, scooters, and people on foot surround her as the convoy slowly lumbers into Pakistan. She is waved through the gates without a pause, and as she speeds up to keep pace, she doesn't try to stop the sobs as the enormity of their decision hits home.

The convoy and Dodge make good time on smoother roads as Sharon watches the sky turning dark and realizes the monsoons have arrived. Two hours into the journey, the trucks pull off the road near a large gas station and dhaba, a roadside tea stall. Sharon turns the car between her and the men before she gets out to stretch. She's slicing an apple when Major Khan walks over.

"Mrs. Singh, we've got new orders and will have to leave you here. I've called a Lahore hotel where army wives stay, and they are expecting you, so no problem." As Sharon reels from this blow, he draws a map to Lahore and the Lotus Hotel. "Stay on the highway; it will take you into town and straight to the Lotus. Signs are in English, so no problem, right-o." He gives a half salute and jogs back to the convoy. Sharon watches the only person she knows by name in the entire country disappear down the road. One hour later, the black clouds open up.

"Imagine driving under a waterfall. The noise was incredible, and I could not see ten feet in front of the car. The windshield wipers couldn't move. I had to pull over, not knowing if I was going into a ditch or a muddy field. My lights were useless."

Sharon sees a darker mass through the curtain of gray water and, thinking it's a building, steers to her right and stops, praying she is off the roadway. Ten minutes go by before the roar of the rain eases. Sharon looks out her left window hoping to see traffic, when someone pounds on the hood. In the thinning rain, two men stand in front of her car, gesturing angrily for her to get out.

"'Like hell,' I thought."

She turns her headlights on, which makes them angrier. The men are in village dress, and each holds a long, heavy wooden staff. Whatever has enraged them, she wants only to back up and leave, but checking her rearview mirror, she sees there are two water buffalo right behind her. If the men would move aside, she could pull onto the highway, but they are furious and raise their poles, like axes, to bring them down on her hood and windshield.

Frantic, she blasts her horn and grabs her pistol, rolling down her window. The horn startles them, giving her time to poke her hand out and fire two shots into the air. They jump back, and she has just enough space to jerk left onto the pavement. She hasn't a clue what angered them, but as she speeds down the open road, Sharon prays they do not have a phone and friends ahead with a car.

"I was physically and emotionally drained. But, Jit was struggling and worried about me, and I'd asked for this, so I had to get through it." Under now clear skies, Sharon sees a sign--Lahore – 37 km--and lets out a whoop of relief.

Jit reaches Kabul that night, but learns the next plane to New Delhi, leaving at 6 a.m., is sold out. He's put on standby and decides to sleep at the airport.

The Lotus Hotel is a colonial leftover, showing its age. But the manager, Mr. Shah, alerted by Major Khan, is welcoming and assures Sharon she can park her car in front of the entrance, solving her worries over its safety. A policeman stands guard at the rear bumper when she comes down later to get a suitcase.

She suspects the big car is a draw for the modest hotel and goes to sleep thinking only of Jit and their reunion.

At 5 a.m., Jit is first on standby and gets his seat on the only flight to New Delhi that day after a nail-biting delay. From the Indian capital, the connecting flight leaves on time for Amritsar at 10 a.m. Jit allows himself to relax a little. Sharon is just a few hours away, God willing.

After an unexpected English breakfast of 'bangers,' fried eggs, toast, and tea, Sharon pays her hotel bill to an exceedingly cheerful Mr. Shah. He's beaming, and his smiling staff stands poised at the door to escort her to the car. Puzzled, but in a rush to get the final fifteen miles over with and see Jit, she hurries out to her muddy blue car that has been transformed.

Her jaw drops as Mr. Shah claps his hands and opens the driver's door with a flourish. The freshly washed and polished Dodge is covered from bumper to bumper with strings of marigolds, and the rows cross over the top, creating a diamond net pattern. It must have taken a dozen people all night.

"It looked like a float in the Rose Parade!" Astonished, Sharon sputters, "Why did you do this, Mr. Shah?"

"For your marriage, of course. You're meeting your groom at the border today, isn't it?" And with that, each hotel employee drapes Sharon with marigold and rose garlands.

Somehow, Sharon's situation was scrambled

during Mr. Shah's English/Urdu conversation with Major Khan. Wedding cars are decorated this way for departing couples. It was a tremendously thoughtful gesture, and Sharon was overwhelmed. She quickly dismisses the idea of taking the flowers off, thinking this may help when she gets to the congested border crossing. She takes out a box of prized sweets, brought for such a moment, and gives them to Mr. Shah with sincere thanks.

As she drives the final miles of their colossal journey, the air is filled with the spicy, aromatic fragrance of marigolds and roses. She laughs as she views the last of Pakistan through the flowers' golden glow.

The border traffic does part for her "wedding" car, as people clap and call out traditional blessings. Even the Indian guards are friendly and pass back her papers with a smile after a quick look inside her trunk. But Sharon's attention is riveted on finding her husband in the masses of people jammed on the Indian side. She coasts along, looking left to right for his familiar turban. Wagah is only twenty miles from the Sikh capital of Amritsar, and dozens of turbaned men surround her. Elation turns to concern as trucks honk to push her along.

Jit arrives by taxi around noon and calculates that Sharon should have beaten him by an hour at least. He checks the parking lot nearest the border, but no Dodge. Deciding to move further away from the cross point, Jit climbs to a restaurant balcony for a better view. There are dozens of cars, trucks, scooters, and tractors. His eyes ignore a marigold-covered lump in the middle of the moving mass. She should be here by now. Jit leans out and scans the vehicles again, searching for a patch of blue. Then, through all the noise of beeping, bleating horns, he hears the familiar, deeper honk of, "'Shave and a haircut.'" That's their signal!

Suddenly, the driver's door of the flower-bedecked car opens, and Jit sees his wife draped in bridal marigolds.

"Hey, handsome, need a lift?"

Days after meeting Sharon that summer and hearing her incredible story, we left for Delhi. Though we returned to Patiala several times over the next six months, we never connected with the couple again.

Gun likely used as protection while driving from Iran to India

"This great Mughal Emperor Akbar was illiterate; he could neither read nor write. However, that had not stopped Akbar from cultivating the acquaintance of the most learned and cultured poets, authors, musicians, and architects of the time – relying solely on his remarkable memory during conversations with them."

Indu Sundaresan

In Any Given Room

We are dinner guests of Ardish Khanna and his wife, Sukriti, in New Delhi in 1983. Khanna hopes my husband, Gopal, will join him in an outsourcing venture, offering maintenance of client files for American attorneys and doctors. It was a popular idea in the early eighties when the Indian business world woke to Western technology's massive potential. Though Gopal is supportive, it is outside his area of interest. Our host graciously concedes defeat, and the evening becomes more social.

I'm meeting Sukriti Khanna for the first time. She's petite, quiet, and keeps her gaze over our shoulders or downcast unless Gopal or I address her directly.

But, as so often happens with Indian women, I sense a bundle of energy waiting for release.

We have a window table in the second-floor dining room of the India International Center. The IIC is a cluster of understated buildings with a small hotel, dining room, and cocktail lounge off an expansive lawn studded with flowering shade trees.

Sukriti has gone to powder her nose, and my thoughts wander while the men visit. An English woman in her late fifties arrives at our table and knows our host well enough to call him by his pet name.

"Bunny, darling, you must introduce me to your new friends. I'm bored silly with the usual suspects tonight."

They chuckle knowingly as our host stands and hugs her. Without waiting for introductions, she walks around to me and takes my hand as Khanna says, "May I present our dear friend Pat, and don't ask her what her real name is. Pat, say hello to Gopal and Indra Kapur from California, and be nice."

"These men are being dull," Pat says. "I saw you were looking out the window, so come with me." Khanna gives us a mock look of displeasure before telling his friend to have me back, "Before the clock strikes twelve, and you turn into a pumpkin."

I'm game, but being aware of our host's wife stops me for a moment. As Pat pulls me up to leave, I look over my shoulder and ask, "Sukriti?" Khanna shakes his head.

"Don't worry; she'll join you shortly." I shrug and give an amused Gopal a hapless wave.

"My full name is Práxedes," Pat volunteers in a soft British accent, "but you call me that, and I'll make you sit through an entire Bollywood movie with sixteen songs." It's an effective threat---I shudder, and we both laugh.

Pat is about 5 feet 10 inches tall, with a figure reminiscent of Jane Russell in her late prime. Wearing a silk caftan in swirls of turquoise and pink and a matching turban studded with sequins and pearls, her march across the dining room with me in tow (in a summer sari of green and white gauzy georgette) has the effect of the Queen Mary II pulling a sailboat as it plows through an Indian fishing village. Waiters stop to watch as heads snap around and chairs are pushed back to get a better look at this sartorial display.

From Pat's right wrist to her elbow, an assortment of metal and glass bangles clang and rattle as she gestures dramatically, throwing back comments on all the people I should meet while I'm in Delhi. I manage only a continuous, amused nod as she weaves us through the tables, and I hold my sari up with my one free hand, hoping to avoid the random foot or chair leg.

We arrive at the lounge where three more British women occupy Pat's corner table. She thrusts me forward, saying, "Look what I found," and introduces me to her friends.

The women tell me they were born in India before independence in 1947, and except for schooling in England and short, futile attempts to live elsewhere ("Canada was boring and cold," says Pat, "and Australia was too dry"), Delhi is their permanent home.

I quickly learn Pat's closest friend, Vicky, named for Queen Victoria, they tell me, with eyes rolling, has a house nearby in the tony Golf Links area. Pat and Vicky live together. The two other women, Muriel and Athena, are sisters who have a bungalow behind a large estate on Ring Road. They speak Hindi fluently and are eccentric, funny, and opinionated; I like them immediately.

Trying to get my measure, Vicky casually asks if I had employed an *ayah* (nanny-servant) for our children when we lived in India for nine months in the early 70s.

"Had I found one with a hygiene I.Q. above believing tap water purified everything, I might have been sorely tempted." The group nods with understanding.

They want to know about California in a humorous, teasing *we don't really, but it gives us a chance to check you out and see if we can tolerate you* kind of way. I give them the short version and am asked the inevitable, "Have you ever seen a movie star?" When I tell them I once met Jerry Lewis and saw Elvis and Richard Burton in person, they lean back and look at each other with a satisfied, "she'll do" nod.

Pat then gaily waves her hand to the waiter, calling out affectionately, "Yusuf, we need attention, dear boy!"

I cringe, wondering what the elderly Muslim must think of this public familiarity. However, he comes over with a sincere smile and bows to her and the table, waiting for our orders.

Pat decides we need Pimm's Cup, a summer drink served with a spear of cucumber, which I forgo with the constant threat of vegetable-borne microbes. Vicky observes me removing the spear and assures me the alcohol will kill any germs.

"Or we would all be dead and buried by now, eh girls?"

"She's right, Indra, except for that time Muriel ended up in hospital with,"-- Pat lowers her voice and leans in close --, "worms. We tell her not to eat from the street vendors, but she thinks she's indestructible. That set your croquet game back a swing or two, eh, Muriel?"

Muriel dismisses the comment with a head toss. "I met that nice Dr. Mehta who pumped my stomach, and he still calls me; you're all just jealous."

I expect a chorus of denials, but the three women look at me, sad-eyed, and wistfully nod in agreement.

Athena, with a long, thin face, black hair cut short, and blunt under a red sequined beret, has a lisp. I give her points for not taking the obvious; *I'm cute with my little-girl lisp.* She chose the sober Keely Smith demeanor, making her lisp much funnier. "Tho," she asks, looking around the room with her heavy-lidded eyes, "what thu you think of New Theli?" She has trouble with the d sound as well.

The table holds its breath waiting, it seems, for me to laugh; *another test?* "I love the city; we lived here for five months in 1971 after moving from Patiala."

They smile in unison, and as Sukriti Khanna comes to the table, hugging and air kissing everyone, Pat and Vicky invite us to a "little soirée" at their home in a week.

"Come at nine," Pat advises. "Nothing worth attending starts before dark in this city. Oh, and wear something comfortable but grand. There will be all kinds there, and we usually end up rolling on the floor at some point." The friends reach over and pat my arm, making "it's not that bad" sounds and then laughing.

I can't wait. I ask if Gopal and Khanna are invited, getting a look of gratitude from Sukriti.

I wonder if I would have reacted differently to the same situation in the States. This has happened before on our travels; an instant friendship between westerners when we meet abroad. I've seen it numerous times in the reverse when Indians approach Gopal in a store or walk across a hotel lobby to talk. We need to connect with the familiar. Perhaps to hear an accent closer to home, to express ourselves and be understood by a kindred spirit in a way a foreigner cannot.

Whatever the cause, I'm glad for the meeting tonight. I find the four women a breath of fresh and animated air. Indian culture is suppressive. When in public with their husbands, fathers, or related males, Indian women are subdued. They hold themselves in, physically and emotionally, often appearing depressed or medicated, which makes any western female in the group look hyper by contrast.

Sukriti, who was quiet and deferential during dinner with the men, came instantly alive with her friends, where she felt free of censure and could be herself. Now, she asks me the questions she has been saving. How many children, how old are they, where do we live in California, how do I like India, and how do I get along with my mother-in-law? Her friends listen quietly, understanding that these are Sukriti's few minutes of freedom.

She enjoys her Pimm's Cup but carefully sets the glass in front of Vicky after each sip in case her husband suddenly appears. The women protect Sukriti, giving her a subtle signal when they see her husband and Gopal approaching. She reins herself in, and Khanna is none the wiser as he places his hand peremptorily on her shoulder. The four Brits are keen observers and caring friends for all their gregariousness and antics. Pat has Khanna pegged and knows that by staying friends with him, Sukriti will be assured of more precious moments to breathe.

A week later, after debating what a "grand" outfit consists of, we arrive by hired car at Pat and Vicky's large home. I wear a beaded, two-piece green silk lungi, which looks Indonesian, but is prevalent in

Southern India and comfortable if we end up rolling around for any legitimate reason.

The circular driveway is bumper to bumper with cars bringing guests. This gathering is more of an event than we realized. As we make our way into the large living room, there are easily fifty people inside, with more spilling out onto a large patio and immaculate English garden. A waiter offers glasses of white wine nicely chilled for a change. Vicky appears at our side and hugs us.

"Don't worry, darlings, it's California Chablis I order by the cartload—friends in low places at the American Embassy. And don't fret about the ice; we boil everything that's not nailed down. So, Gopal, we do have scotch if you like."

Most Indians have a phobia about chilled drinks in the summer, convinced they cause colds and sore throats. We avoid ice if we don't know the water source, so Vicky's assurance is appreciated.

As Gopal moves to the bar, sisters Athena and Muriel gaily welcome him. Vicky introduces me to Sanjay Khosla, an older, elegantly dressed man in a summer linen Nehru jacket. As she turns to greet other guests, he shakes my hand, an indicator that he's traveled outside of India. He asks how I know "the girls," and I tell him how we met as he and I watch Pat sailing about the room, leaning in for a confidence here, clinking glasses there, waving to new arrivals, before she sees us and gives a "be right there" signal.

As I sip my wine and look over the crowd, there's a familiar face in the throng. Yusuf, the waiter from IIC, is a guest. His presence is somewhat unusual, and I ask Khosla about him.

"Ah, Yusuf's daughter, Shabana, was married to a rogue whose family treated her quite badly, threatening to turn her out if Yusuf and his wife didn't provide more dowry money. Pat and the girls organized a protest march and raised a ruckus. The press loved the fuss, and then friends in parliament got involved and passed yet another dowry bill. Little real meaning, of course, but symbolically, it meant something. While public sympathy was high, Shabana got a divorce and eventually found a worthy husband. You can understand; Yusuf was deeply grateful."

"Do you know Yusuf's daughter?" I ask.

"Yes, of course. Shabana is just there, in the yellow sari, chatting with Sukriti Khanna. She returned to college in the U.K. and is now a divorce attorney, representing only women."

I follow his gaze and see a striking, confident woman deep in conversation with Sukriti.

Resettling his eyes on Pat, Sanjay murmurs, "She's quite amazing, you know."

I look at him expectantly, hoping for more, but he continues watching her with a melancholy gaze.

"You and Pat are old friends?"

"Yes, dear friends." He smiles with irony. "We fell in love a lifetime ago and were married secretly before mixed marriages were allowed. My mother was orthodox and attempted suicide. Pat's father sent her to England after a hush-hush annulment, and I was packed off to the army."

After a long moment of studying his wine glass, he continues. "I had to accept an arranged marriage to a woman of my parents' choosing." His eyes caress Pat, and sensing him, she turns, and for a moment, they are alone in the room.

This revelation is in a calm, "it's too late for us" voice, and I can only watch as Pat, with Gopal in tow, joins us and introduces my husband to the man she loves but cannot have.

After exchanging greetings, Gopal and I make our way to the garden perfumed with tuber roses and frangipani trees. As I tell him Pat and Sanjay's story, not for the first time do we appreciate how lucky we are.

Despite resistance to our marriage in the form of a private detective following me for four months and harassing calls from an older Indian cousin in Massachusetts questioning Gopal's sanity, it finally ended in San Francisco, where a trusted family friend was visiting from India and agreed to meet me. Only then was a reluctant nod given by Gopal's parents.

It took several more years of stumbles and misses before my in-laws accepted me and finally grew fond of me to some degree. Though one of Gopal's aunts still refuses to be civil the few times we meet.

Pat never got the same chance. She was British in a country struggling to get the British out. Despite his

Oxford education and wealth, Sanjay was considered unworthy. Indians were banned from their buildings and public grounds by the occupying British. An Indian marrying an English woman in those turbulent times was unthinkable, though more than a few British men had Indian 'wives' and children discreetly tucked away.

Muriel comes to usher us in for the entertainment. "See the man sitting on the rug in the corner? That's Firoz Khan, the Yehudi Menuhin of the saroad. With eight strings, it has a deeper sound than the sitar. His father was famous and performed for the Royal Family at Albert Hall in London. Firoz was chained to the instrument as a child and forced to practice for hours. You'll notice his second finger is much longer than normal, stretched while still growing, and now deformed. He's brilliant. Get a pillow seat near to him before I do the introductions."

We find two silk cushions and settle in. Khan is introduced and then begins to pluck, rather than strum, the strings. The music is hauntingly beautiful. After a while, I hear women singing and look around, expecting to see a chorus. But there is only a roomful of people riveted on this gifted musician. He plays a morning raga, light and quick, followed by a gentle, melancholy evening raga, a favorite of his hostess, Pat.

After asking for a glass of water, in a deep, melodious voice, he tells a story about his annual trek alone on the back of a donkey up into the high hills that shoulder the Himalayas. He always goes alone, he explains, with only a second donkey carrying his saroad. There, he finds a flat rock and spends a week playing for the sadhus--mystics from several faiths who sleep in caves and sit for hours in the nude, bodies smeared with ash, fasting and praying to assorted gods.

There are several encores before Khan gets up and acknowledges the sustained applause. We step forward to thank him for the beautiful performance. I mention the women singing, and he smiles, delighted.

"Ah, sometimes, when the conditions are right, and I'm in top form"-- his eyes close as he relishes the thought -- "the sounds build in my saroad in such a way that the music sails out around the room, and you hear singing. It is wonderful, isn't it?" We assure him indeed it is, as he namastes in farewell.

Later, as we talk with Vicky and Athena, I notice a blond woman speaking intimately with Khan. Curious, I ask Vicky who she is.

"Oh, that's Felicity, Firoz's long-time mistress from London. She produces his concerts on the BBC. He moved her into his family home in Calcutta for three months at one point. That's a side of him we loathe, but what can anyone do? This part of the world looks the other way. He's brilliant and incorrigible." "Hidiouth!" Athena adds.

I can only imagine the pain of disgrace and humiliation Khan's wife endured as the neighborhood servants, friends, and relatives in Calcutta became aware of the blond mistress settling into the family home.

Sanjay is holding Pat's hands in an alcove near the front door as we hug our final good night after inviting the friends to visit us in California. I'm moved by the evening as we walk to our car. The deep friendships and enduring love, the loyalties and betrayals, the egos and genius, the still waters and the shallows, one seldom knows the myriad undercurrents in any given room.

"It is a great act of cleverness to be able to conceal one's being clever."

Francois de La Rochefoucauld

A Man of Few Words

During a winter visit to India in the 80s with my husband, Gopal, I first met Mr. Shastri. He was a friend of my husband's parents and would drop in several times a week for a chat and a cup of tea.

In Indian society, there are several levels of visits. Neighbors and acquaintances stopping by before lunch understand it's too early for tea. Popping in after lunch but before official 'tea time' may get you a small cup of tea, but no snacks. Many people take a nap, run errands, or start preparing dinner during this time of day, so these visits are short and to the point. Once official tea time begins, between four and six in the afternoon, you get the complete treatment.

A servant may run to buy hot snacks from the corner shop.

Tea (always cooked with milk) will be abundant and served with an assortment of little bowls filled with cashews, dried fruit, peanuts, and almonds. As the recipient of this hospitality, you're expected to visit as though you have nothing more important to do. Telling amusing stories will only enhance your reputation as a good guest.

Mr. Shastri was someone who transcended all these levels. He was so well-liked by my father and mother-in-law that he would come before breakfast, after lunch, or anytime between, and a cup of tea with snacks was instant.

On a visit in the late 90s, as we were finishing breakfast, Shastri's familiar soft rap was heard at the back door, and he was invited to join us. Gopal's younger brother, Kris, was also visiting from California, and they began chatting about yoga. It surprised us to learn that Shastri taught yoga, and before long, he and Kris were sitting bare-chested on the back lawn, doing warm-up exercises in the bracing December fog.

Several days later, he came for his usual early morning visit. The weather was freezing, with fog patches hugging the ground, and no one could decide if it was warmer outside or inside. Most homes in India do not have central heating, so people bundle and layer to keep warm.

Shastri's solution, along with a heavy sweater and hand-knitted woolen gloves, was a curious cotton cap more appropriate for an infant. The hat looked like a miniature hooked rug. Little yellow cotton tufts stood up over this dignified man's head. No one else found this comical. I struggled to keep from laughing as I helped arrange chairs and then escaped to make tea.

I became fond of Mr. Shastri but only from a distance. He was from an older generation of Indian men who found having the usual give-and-take conversation with a younger woman nearly impossible. Add that I was foreign and spoke English with an accent and speed he found incomprehensible, and it left us with only polite nods of hello and goodbye.

One day, on the rare occasion I was home alone, Shastri knocked on the door—we would have to talk now, but I felt sympathy for his ingrained discomfort. By keeping the screen door between us, he could not see me, and by turning his head to one side as he spoke, he was not conversing either.

I told him when the family would return, and he murmured something and left. Later that day, he returned with a small bag in his hand, and I assumed it was a snack he sometimes brought for everyone to have with tea.

Leaving the men to chat at the dining table, I returned to my book but was called within minutes to rejoin them. Gopal handed me a magnifying glass and a clear plastic container the size of a large biscuit. I glanced at Shastri, who was looking about two feet north of my shoulder, a little smile on his lips.

Under the clear lid was a grain of white rice glued at its tip to the end of a pin which was itself glued to the inside rim of the container. This clever arrangement allowed us to view the grain of rice from all sides. Under the magnifier, in a beautiful, precise script, were the words *Merry Christmas, Gopal and Indra Kapur, 1998.*

To write a typical sentence freehand on unlined paper and keep a straight line would be a challenge because, by the late 90s, Shastri was nearing his 80s. To do this on a grain of rice, perfectly spaced and tremor-free, was phenomenal. Our effusive appreciation and genuine praise were met with shyness, a soft "thank you," and a quick retreat to the lawn chairs where he continued his visit with my father-in-law.

The following year he gave us another rice grain with our children's names and birthdates. All questions of how he did this were met with an enigmatic smile.

Shastri was a retired engineer and a widower. His only child, a daughter, had moved home with her husband to care for her father. This arrangement sounded ideal, but we wondered why, in all these years, my father-in-law, himself recently widowed, had never been invited to his friend's house for tea since Shastri was living in his own home. But then, that was the irony in the tragedy of Mr. Shastri.

Gopal's father finally visited his friend because Shastri became gravely ill. What he found was heartbreaking. This gentle, kind man was confined to a small room no bigger than a walk-in closet. His clothes, books, and a few possessions were stacked and wedged precariously to the ceiling of this tiny space in the corner of his own home. There was barely room to squeeze into the cot where he lay neglected and semi-conscious.

His daughter and her nefarious husband had commandeered the home, forcing Shastri into a virtual cell, and then sat waiting for him to die. Before my father-in-law left, he promised to bring a doctor and medicine.

I asked why we couldn't just bring him to our house and nurse him ourselves. No, Gopal explained, that would infuriate his daughter, showing her up for what she was, and once he returned home, there would be hell to pay.

I never saw him again. He died in his little room a few days later, probably cold and alone. Gopal and his father (women are not allowed) went to the cremation and paid a brief visit to the daughter and son-in-law.

After a few minutes of stilted grief, the son-in-law, thinking he was speaking with like-minded men, expressed frustration in not finding Shastri's will. Indian courts are backlogged with inheritance cases, and survivors often begin fighting over property immediately after death.

Gopal's father, though long retired, was an attorney before becoming a political science professor and then a college president. He told the man that this was not an appropriate time and changed the subject. The daughter, coming into the room at that moment, hadn't heard the discussion. She carried a bundle tied with a cord and handed it to Gopal, saying, "These are things my father wanted your father to have." Then, oblivious to the tension in the room, she asked in a whining tone if her father had ever mentioned where he had put his will.

The previous weeks of seeing these two mistreat their friend were too much. Gopal and his father got up and walked out.

His friend's death deeply saddened my father-in-law. Within two years, he had lost his wife of 63 years and one of his closest and oldest friends. We had to fly home three weeks later and did not return to India for ten months.

On the next visit, remembering Shastri and his endearing ways, I recalled the little bundle.

"What did he want you to have?" I asked my father-in-law.

"Oh, I don't know," he said and ended the discussion with a dismissive wave. It was still painful to remember how his friend had died.

A few days later, I found the bundle while replacing towels in the linen closet, and Gopal decided we should open it. There were books and poems they had both liked, Shastri's pocket watch, and a familiar clear plastic case.

My father-in-law was sitting in a patch of winter sunlight, reading the paper, when Gopal carried out the magnifying glass and the case. He saw what it was and started to push it away, but Gopal said, "No, Dad, you need to see this."

He held the glass over the tiny grain of rice and read the words: To B.K. Kapur, I leave all my property and goods. Lal Shastri, Jan.10, 2004.

Though the daughter and son-in-law vehemently protested, the court ruled the will valid and authentic. The judge reasoned that no one but Mr. Shastri himself could have written those words on a grain of rice. The 'tenants' were given six months to find other accommodations, and then Mr. Shastri's home became a preparatory school for poor children who wanted to become engineers.

"A man wrapped up in himself makes a very small package."

John Ruskin

The VIP Function

January 2009

Gopal and I have been in Patiala, Northern India, for two months and are still housebound without consistent wheels. Two days back, we got out, but it was programmed to the minute by my father-in-law. Yet another function, this time at Gopal's old high school, became a battle of nerves and patience.

VIPs and other chief guests get the attention, and too little goes to the children. Those seated on stage and in the two front rows receive refreshments in full view of long-suffering faculty and students. But Friday's event was over the top.

To reach the assembly, we enter through a regular-sized doorway amid stores and shops. A hallway about thirty feet long leads into a large courtyard that now holds the entire student body. Lining the hallway on both sides were eight little girls around seven years old dressed in white frocks, with lacy headdresses and white veils.

Someone saw Holy Communion dresses and copied them in minute detail. Every third child in these two lines was a young boy in khaki shorts and a white shirt, holding a flute, and one older boy had a snare drum. On the hall's red carpet, written in flower petals, was "WELCOME."

When we entered with my father-in-law, the flutes blew at full blast, there was a drum roll, and the girls showered us with petals. Three hundred fifty students inside, seated on the courtyard floor, whistled and cheered. Then someone realized we were not the Chief VIP guests, and the music died away.

Before we left the house, I again stated my case about not being seated on the stage, nor did I want to pass out awards or sweaters. At these functions, I find the attention lavished on the givers at the expense of the children offensive.

We did succeed in staying off the stage. We finally convinced everyone that we did not need or want a trophy (Gopal's father proudly has over thirty lining his living room), and we would prefer the money to go for books and paper. At first, we got confused looks, but now it's reluctantly understood.

The biggest VIP and Chief Guest in charge of this network of schools, coming from Chandigarh, a 45-minute drive, was over an hour late. The little girls in their thin dresses and flower baskets, the flute boys, and the drummer all stood at attention in the cold hallway, waiting for this insufferable dolt. So did the 350-plus rest of us. Tea was served every 30 minutes to those on stage and the first two rows while the children and faculty could only watch.

Whenever a guest arrived that the greeting children mistook for the VIP, we would hear the flutes and drum start up, then quickly die away. Finally, the man walked in with much harrumphing from the gallery and bowing and scraping from the principal. The master of ceremonies, a senior male teacher, introduced everyone in row one, emphasizing Gopal's father since he has given much to the school in recent years.

The first row, minus Gopal and me, was called on stage for even more critical seat positioning. This gave lesser VIPs a chance to move up, and a new group quickly surrounded us. On stage, there were over sixty medium and small trophies on a side table for high achievers in the student body. Thirty children in costumes peeked out from behind multiple cloth walls. I tried not to think of the fire hazard but failed when there was a flickering four-candle prayer and marigold altar in one corner.

Just as Gopal returned to his seat after presenting sweaters to fifty students, accompanied by a DJ playing western music on a Casio keyboard, the electricity went off.

Here is where western and Indian planning part company. Americans, knowing this happens almost every day, would have a generator (with a backup) standing by. Teachers, led by our fearless principal, and four lesser VIPs, approach the DJ and launch into an animated discussion of what to do. Finally, an underling (who does all the grunt work and knows where everything is) is ordered to get a generator. One tea-drenched hour later, with a mile of electrical cable and wiring trailing through the crowd, the lights, music, and microphones come back on.

An adorable troupe of costumed nine-year-old girls had just assembled on stage when the power went off. They were left there for over twenty minutes while the men, shocked at the power failure, puzzled over their dilemma.

This program started at 1 p.m. By 3:45, we were not even close to the sixty trophies or the numerous dance groups patiently waiting back tent. Gopal and I had to meet a painting contractor at the orphanage where we were getting repairs done. We left with little danger of notice since people had been moving ever closer to the stage and were now packed shoulder to shoulder. We had to step over numerous adults and children to get to the hall. My father-in-law wanted us back in time to hear his speech in Punjabi.

The children were adorable, had practiced for weeks, and did an excellent job, but there was no end.

We finally got away at 6 p.m., and there were still acts waiting to go on.

Several qualities are present in Indian children and teens that I sorely miss in the US--politeness to each other and adults and patience in the face of problems.

Most of the students were boys from first grade up to high school. With the delays and crowded conditions in a US school, a dozen fights would have broken out. Nothing close to that happened, except between the person who designed the women's restroom and me, but that's another story.

"In the best of times there is nothing simple about an Indian boarding a train."

Paul Theroux

Platform 8

There are only three ways to get to Patiala, 160 miles north of New Delhi. My husband, Gopal, and I can hire a car with a driver and, for six excruciating hours, endure one of the three most dangerous highways in the world, or we can take a bus that may decide to skip our stop, or we can take the train.

The savvy traveler buys a first-class ticket with air conditioning, a cut above the basic first-class car. Since we're only there in winter, we can glance up and see the numerous unplugged fans attached to our a/c car's ceiling as we roll along. In a/c first class, we also have our choice of western or Indian bathroom facilities and windows permanently sealed shut. This luxury can be had for around seventeen dollars per person. Since our first trip together in 1971, we had boarded the train from the nether world of the main

New Delhi Station. Then, three years ago, the platform to board our Bathinda Express was changed to number one, moving us from the back of acres of tracks, stairs, sky bridges, and hundreds of rushing people to the very first platform out of the station's door.

We usually have three 50-pound suitcases, each carried by a coolie who walks faster than an athlete and has been known to abscond with your belongings, as the locals say. To stop the growing problem of luggage theft, a new rule was decreed that every red-shirted coolie must wear an armband with a brass plate engraved with the coolie's registration number. The first thing Gopal does is ask to see their plate numbers.

Last January, we rested in Delhi after a 23-hour flight from California, plus a 12-hour fog delay in Frankfurt, Germany. Gopal made his routine call from our hotel to confirm the train's departure time and learned, to our dismay, that our train would be leaving from the Old Delhi Station because of remodeling on the central station.

The old station is 60 minutes from our hotel, and the facilities are archaic. Our taxi driver could not pull in close due to broken bricks and rubble strewn around the station's entrance. Gopal did his usual astute bartering and banter with the dozen coolies who saw me, a westerner, and homed in on us like hyenas to a kill.

My husband has a clear sense of coolies who will stick with us if the train is delayed (we need their muscle to lift our bags onto the racks above our seats) or will abandon us to fend for ourselves. Gopal chose three men; one young with a smirk for every request and two over 50 years old. One was tall (we could find him in the teeming crowds), and their leader, Benny, who was the eldest, smallest, and smartest.

As I feared, our platform was eight tracks away at this older station. We had to climb and descend two sets of stairs, keep up with our trotting coolies who balanced our bags on their heads, and dodge and weave through rushing crowds of people descending the stairs three and four abreast as fast as possible.

The citizens of India do not value or observe public order. There are no left-right protocols on stairs or "enter" and "exit" doors on train cars—why drag logic into the equation? It's always a shoving, pushing, squeezing match between crowds of opposing forces and the part of the experience I loathe. I've been saved from injury by being obviously foreign and thereby getting a little elbow room at critical moments.

We reach platform eight, at last, only to find the one metal bench in sight taken with a family eating their picnic lunch and surrounded by assorted bags, bedrolls, and large tea thermoses. I stand as close as possible, ready to sit if anyone gets up. Passengers hurry past with pull cases in tow, banging into or rolling over anything in their paths.

The occasional beggar child sidles up, so I always carry candies. These children are hardened professionals, and as much as I want to hand them a five or ten rupee note, I dare not. Word would quickly spread, and we'd be surrounded in minutes.

A long sleeper train to Mumbai is parked behind us. I soon realize my clever plan not to need a restroom until I'm on board has failed me. There are no public toilets on these platforms, and I would have to hurry back to the main building by myself. This is not an option for the simple reason that our train could arrive at any moment. Electronic boards with arrivals and departures do not work, nor can we understand the female announcer's muffled voice. Our best source of information is our head coolie, and we watch Benny for any clue.

I notice women hopping onto the parked sleeper train and, minutes later, hopping off. Of course, they're using the train's restrooms. I risk the trip several times but am so afraid the train will start moving out that I give up and grit my teeth. A younger me could have jumped from a slow-moving train but no longer.

Two hours go by, and halfway through, I finally get to sit down when the family leaves. Gopal moves around the area, confirming with other passengers that this is the right platform. No one is certain because locations can change when there's fog and trains start backing up miles out—as is now the case with our Bathinda Express.

Soon, another fuzzy announcement is heard, and we see our coolies rushing to lift our bags. The men speak Hindi, so I read faces and wait until everything is said before asking what's happening. We must move to platform one, as our train is due in ten minutes!

This goes for the other fifty-plus people waiting with us, and there's a stampede to the nearest stairs. We look to see a solid block of people stuck as everyone pushes the protesting travelers in front to move up the choked stairway.

Benny gestures decisively to follow him in the opposite direction. I'm alarmed; had he misheard the announcement? One other person is now in our little group, a man from Canada visiting his family in Patiala after 15 years. With his coolie, seven of us are scrambling to keep up with our head man, who rushes off, then abruptly stops in front of a wall on the platform made of tangled rebar, steel mesh, and clumps of wires.

Our coolie sets our bag down and reaches through the bars and wires to push a hidden button, and like Ali Baba's secret door, the wall lifts to reveal the oldest, most decrepit elevator platform I have ever seen. There's no time to marvel at this contraption as Benny shouts to hurry; our train is pulling in!

We are pushed and packed, seven people and four huge suitcases with our carry-on bags, along with a tiny, grizzled man I hadn't noticed before. He is calmly saying something to no one in particular, and the coolies are angrily shouting at him.

He operates the lift, and we're not going anywhere until he's paid ten rupees. Gopal gladly hands it over (about 22 cents), knowing we would have happily paid a hundred-fold if he had asked. I expect us to ascend to the sky bridge, but we start going down. Everyone is talking as the creaking, groaning elevator, unable to handle the weight, slowly sinks.

In my worst claustrophobic nightmare, this is where we will die, trapped cheek to jowl in a dark elevator with a million tons of steel overhead. The coolies are shouting in Hindi as I close my eyes, biting back panic. Gopal somehow finds my arm in the dark and explains that we're okay. A tunnel below will lead us to our train by-passing the crowds and stairs. Before I can celebrate this reprieve, the door slides up, and we are hustled out and told to run!

Our bags are quickly piled onto a rough wooden cart circa tenth century India, which they push in front of them over a raw dirt floor covered in construction rubble. The tunnel would have fit perfectly into any escape movie ever made. A few single low-wattage bulbs are strung along one wall, giving us minimal light to see. The Indian from Canada is shouting behind me as we run, "I'm never coming back, I'm never coming back!"

Overhead, the continuous deep rumble of trains on the move adds to the anxiety. We get to the opposite side and find a matching gnarled and twisted metal door that opens to another "ten rupees."

Gopal pays, and up we slowly go to one of the exceedingly rare miracles of efficiency in India. Benny delivered us to our a/c car, and we stepped off the elevator and walked onto our train. The relief was breathtaking.

**Old Delhi train station,
coolie with brass arm plate**

"There are three trips you take to India: the one you think you're going to have – that you plan for; the one you actually have; and the one you live through once you go back home."

Erin Reese

The Last Option

It happened in Cambridge, Massachusetts, as my husband Gopal and I were walking through a genteel neighborhood on our way to tour the home of the poet, Longfellow. As we stepped off a curb, a young woman dressed in slacks and a crisp white blouse approached us on a ten-speed bicycle.

I can still recall my quick impression of her, about twenty-three years old, chubby, and wearing a new pair of tennis shoes. There was an air of entitlement that was reinforced by her tone of voice. Without taking her hands off the handlebars, she invoked her two absent and hungry children and asked us for money.

What I said to her would trouble me for a long time. To this young woman, I responded with, "You could sell your bike." She probably wasn't expecting rejection in this neighborhood, just blocks from Harvard and MIT, and she shot back with, "Wow, that's harsh."

Gopal was aghast. My family knows me as an incorrigible soft touch. She sped off as I began asking myself, why was I angry with her? The answer would come years later, from a source I could not have imagined.

Whenever we visit Gopal's hometown of Patiala, India, we enjoy shopping in the colorful and chaotic bazaar. Like old bazaars everywhere, it is a mishmash of streets, alleys, and narrow lanes that are added when needed, with no design or thought to the future. It's dangerous for people on foot, with cars and fast scooters shoving through the tangle of rickshaws, three-wheeler taxis, and bicycles.

Our favorite shops are bordered by a lane too narrow for anything but foot traffic. Open drains are common in India, and one crossed this lane. Someone, perhaps a store owner, had done a half-hearted job of partially covering it, so potential customers did not have to hop over the continuous stream of offal. Now there was a little bridge of sorts, no more than two feet by two feet, where the path narrowed. On busy days people would stand aside for a moment and let others pass before continuing.

We were coming down the lane one day when I saw the beggar for the first time. He sat on the right of the little bridge in an impossibly tiny space, but exactly where we would have to pause to let others pass. He could hear us coming, and when we stopped, he raised his cup a few inches from the ground and, with a gentle humming, asked for help.

Over the next several wintertime trips to India, we came to expect his presence. He was always in the same place, but we never saw him arrive or leave nor saw any conveyance. Someone had to bring him there and carry him away at night.

He had long since lost his ability to walk because his feet were gone. He could barely lift the battered cup because his fingers were reduced to stubs. His face was cruelly distorted, and he was blind. All that remained of his voice was the ability to quietly call out with the groaning hum that ended in a few mumbled words of appeal. What was left of his wretched body was inside a bundle of rags that just managed to cover him and provide a bit of warmth.

Leprosy was almost finished with him, but somehow he hung on.

I quietly marveled at the cleverness of this man. In all of Patiala, he had found the one perfect place for his multitude of handicaps. He had chosen a narrow lane safe from cars, scooters, rickshaws, and bikes, plus the loose cattle roaming at will. People had to pause at this spot to cross the bridge, and all one had to do was reach down and drop money in his cup.

We gave him enough for the day's meals each time, but no more, for he would probably be robbed. He remained passive, barely making himself known if you didn't look at him, and few people did. Over many visits, we never saw anyone put money in his cup. So what, I wondered, brought him back, day after day?

No one sane person in a billion would change places with him. A leper in India, with all his senses gone but a scrape of voice and hearing; his face destroyed, his limbs dissolving, alone and reviled, and yet, there was more to him than just a beggar's cup.

He had one option left, and few would blame him for taking the final step. But incredibly, this man, carrying this horrific burden, suffering beyond our comprehension, retained a shred of dignity and hope. He believed he still had a purpose and was not ready to lie down and die.

In America, we don't like to think any of us has to beg, so we use the ambiguous word panhandling to dress up what should be a desperate, last-ditch act of dire need, to be used only when all else fails.

Had all else failed for the Cambridge beggar? In one of the most affluent and family-friendly states in the US, it would take her years to bounce out of all the safety nets Massachusetts provided before she even thought about going to the streets for survival.

That day, her behavior mocked the millions of people who have run out of options, who will never know what a safety net looks like, and who will never walk or ride a bicycle again. She disgraced us as a people, and I had been ashamed.

On our visit last year, the beggar was not there. Someone enlarged his tiny spot, and an orange seller's cart occupied the space. We went down the lane several times, but he was gone. We asked the nearest shop owner if he knew what happened to him, but a beggar's whereabouts didn't warrant a response beyond a shrug of disgust. "Probably at the leper colony," the orange seller offered.

As I heard this, I wondered where the Cambridge beggar was that day.

Taking her children to the park, or having lunch on a bench by the Charles River, watching the Harvard rowing teams practice?

The Patiala beggar, who had perhaps once laughed and danced, who had held a job and had dreams for the future, lay dying, with all options spent.

"I was getting tired of the Asiatic inquisition: Where do you come from? What do you do? Married or single? Any children? This nagging made me evasive, secretive, foolish, an inventor of cock-and-bull stories."

Paul Theroux, **The Great Railway Bazaar**

Dinner With Mr. Kirkehz

Several years ago, while visiting a government conference and teaching center in New Delhi, India, my husband Gopal and I were invited by the center's director to an evening reception in honor of a visiting VIP.

I'm familiar with India and her ways, and I know that the who and why of the occasion (details vital to a westerner) are less critical than Director Rao's gesture of simply inviting us. *All will be revealed in due time* should be stamped on every visitor's visa to this complex country.

We arrive at the aptly named VIP dining room, where two waiters offer drinks and hors d'oeuvres.

The room is rectangular, with a long, low table in the middle, surrounded by even lower cushioned chairs that tip back, like a leaning L. Once you sit down, there is no graceful way to get up.

Trained in American promptness, we are the second and third guests to arrive at the appointed time in a country that struggles with the concept. The first is a jovial Indian man visiting from his home in Southern California. We laugh about our shared 'affliction' as other guests slowly trickle in.

Being fashionably late is a social sport held dear by many people worldwide and practiced at Olympian levels in India. At parties, dinner is sometimes served around midnight because the last guests typically don't arrive until after ten. The idea of serving dinner for the good of those who did arrive on time is never a consideration. If the mystery guest of honor this night is Indian, we could be having our dessert well past one o'clock in the morning.

An hour after the suggested time for cocktails, Rao steps into the room to herald the arrival of the VIP. There are now about a dozen people assembled, all wisely still standing. The group comprises senior professors from the center, the mayor of Delhi, the editor of *Femina Magazine*, and Mr. Malik, India's former ambassador to Spain.

With a slight bow and extended arm to usher him into the room, Rao introduces the First Secretary of Sikandarstan, who is preceded by his bodyguard and trailed by his translator. The guard gives the guests the twice-over, who then retreats to a chair in the corner farthest from the only entrance to the room.

The novel thought occurs that if an assassin barges in, intent on the First Secretary, the bodyguard will have the entire group of people between him and the culprit. True, there could be a master plan of defense known only to them, but I thought you were to stay very close to the body you were guarding.

Everyone is urged to be seated, and Gopal and I end up directly across from the First Secretary and his translator. Introductions are made across the table, and we quickly learn that a lot is riding on the First Secretary's shoulders. He hands us his card with an Ernest Borgnine smile, enhanced by two gold front teeth.

In addition to being the "First Secretary of Sikandarstan Democratic Party Political Council," he's the "First Vice-Chair of the Movement-National Revival of Sikandarstan, Deputy of Sikandarstan Mejlis, Doctor of Philosophic Sciences, Academician, member of Sikandarstan Academy of Sciences, Professor." These titles take all the space on the card, save for a tiny corner spot for the Sikandarstan flag. His email address and phone numbers are on the back. This evening, however, we may call him simply Mr. Kirkehz.

His Indian translator speaks English with an odd mix of British, Indian, and Slavic accents. He tells us he studied in Russia and is originally from Kerala, a southern, coastal state distinctive for being one of the most beautiful, having the highest literacy rate (93%)

in India and the highest percentage of Communists. Apparently, these two sons of the hammer and sickle, now seated across from us, failed to attend Gorbachev's seminar on "Why This Isn't Working For Us Anymore."

As soon as everyone has a drink, Mr. Kirkehz gives our host, Mr. Rao, an effusive toast with the requisite clinking of glasses. The director returns the toast and starts conversations with people nearer to him. Mr. Kirkehz, however, is just warming up and rises in his chair to declare a toast to India and her people.

The translator's eyes are darting back and forth, taking in everyone's inattention as conversations grow louder. Only former Ambassador Malik, to my left, and Gopal and I, across from Kirkehz, keep our glasses at the ready for the next clink.

We know that toasting is a big part of the social protocol in Kirkehz's country, and return toasts are expected to be with equal or greater enthusiasm. Our director host is oblivious, and we cannot take up the toasting slack since we are not part of the official host group.

Kirkehz is uneasy and well on his way to being insulted. If he reminds me of Earnest Borgnine, his translator is Peter Lorre, without the sly smile. Mr. Lorre is now very nervous and starts smoothing down his well-oiled hair with his left hand while his sad eyes scan the room, looking for an escape hatch. The bodyguard suddenly gets up, walks to his boss, and as he leans down to whisper, Gopal and I catch a glimpse of his gun, snugly held in a shoulder holster.

The guard seems to calm the First Secretary, who settles down in his chair with a resigned smile.

In rapid-fire chatter, Mr. Malik turns my way and tells me about his four years in Washington, D.C., when he was with India's Embassy before becoming an ambassador. I ask if his wife will join us (people are still drifting in) "yes, yes, yes," he replies. She's attending a local stage production of, *Who's Afraid of Virginia Woolf,* and should be right along. He asks me if we have children, and I give him their ages and marital status.

This personal information is routinely exchanged at the start of all local social gatherings. I have long since overcome the 'none of your business' feelings I struggled with years ago.

Gopal leans over to the translator, who has broken out in flop sweat, and asks Mr. Kirkehz what a typical dinner would be for a Sikandarstan family. Why, the ever-popular bar-be-cued camel with curd, of course. We then receive an invitation to dine with his Excellency when we visit his country.

Since he is still being ignored by most of the table, we press on with another question; what is the current price of gasoline? Indians pay $4.75 per gallon. He tells us that his fellow citizens pay only seven cents a liter (28 cents a gallon). Gopal wonders under his breath why they don't just give it away. Huge oil reserves were discovered about 20 years ago, so for the first time in her history, Sikandarstan is the bell of the international oil ball, and India is smitten.

Kirkehz comments that he must return home for the national elections in two days. I can't resist asking this First Secretary of the Democratic Party Political Council how many political parties participate in the election. His translator looks over my shoulder into the middle distance and says, "one." We are saved by a small bell as the group is called to an excellent Chinese buffet in the lobby.

With our first taste of Mandarin prawns, Mrs. Malik sweeps into the room, greets the director, and briefly confers with her husband. Two minutes later, she slides into a chair next to Gopal and spends 15 seconds on chit-chat before asking if our son is available as a possible match for their 29-year-old daughter. Gopal does a perfect ten in verbal gymnastics, but her attention span can't hold up, and she quickly moves on, despite the chair, to greener prospects.

As the dinner reception draws to a close at 11:00 p.m., we say goodbye to Mr. Kirkehz and wish him a safe journey back to petrol heaven. We learn that he addressed energy officials the following day and was then escorted to the airport by a dozen of India's elite and heavily armed Black Berets.

India's Prime Minister announced a joint effort with Pakistan to build a massive oil pipeline system from Sikandarstan, to supply both countries with this much-needed commodity. After hearing the news, Gopal and I toasted Mr. Kirkehz's success with gusto.

"Only in the darkness can you see the stars."

Dr. Martin Luther King, Jr.

Mukhtar's Honor

On December 10, 2008, as my husband Gopal and I waited for a table at a local restaurant in Northern California, I picked up a discarded page from the Sacramento Bee. A small story caught my eye. A woman was to speak the following night at the Sacramento Hilton, but we had tickets the same evening for a Christmas dinner dance, a rare night out. After Gopal read the piece, he agreed that we would not be going to a dance.

In 2002, a story came across the news wires that ripped my heart. In a small village in northeastern Pakistan, Shakur, a tall boy of twelve, was seen walking with an unmarried woman of twenty. Despite the age difference, gossip quickly spread that the woman's honor had been compromised.

The woman's powerful clan, the Mostoi, took the matter to the *panchayat*, the village's illiterate judge and jury of four like-minded men. Shakur's father was called to the 'trial.' After deliberation, the sentence was announced.

Honor would be restored to the Mostoi by having their men rape Shakur's unmarried older sister, 25. This news was delivered to the sister by her weeping father and brothers. They were powerless to save her as she was led to a village barn by her father. He and her older brothers could only wait, along with 200 men of the village, while she was attacked in the barn by men she knew and had grown up around. The crowd jeered her as she was shoved out of the barn half naked and in shock. Her father and uncle lead her home.

Rape victims in Pakistan are expected to commit suicide. The Mostoi assumed their little problem would disappear within a day or two. Her name is Mukhtar Mai, and she is speaking the next night at the Hilton.

Today, the titles of hero and heroine are often given with abandon. Complete your re-hab, hit a grand slam, lose 100 lbs., or give part of an extensive financial portfolio away, with press coverage, and you're a hero.

We get two of the last four tickets, including the pre-dinner reception. Two hundred fifty people are attending, and I want very much to meet her. The early reception includes a copy of her book and a photo taken with Mukhtar. She enters with two local

Pakistani women and stands unnoticed in the middle of the room. Class lines are rigid in their culture, and rape victims are always pariahs. The two women are wives of Sacramento attorneys. In Pakistan, they would never acknowledge her existence, much less speak with Mukhtar.

She is quickly escorted to a photographer's dark backdrop, where the picture-taking begins. When it's my turn, I address her in Urdu with the traditional Muslim greeting; she replies. I take her hand and thank her for being extraordinarily courageous, fighting the thugs, and telling her story. A countryman stands near her translating. She nods, smiling slightly, hands me her book, and then it's the next person's turn.

It is easy to overstate the experience, so when I say I was in the presence of greatness, I have considered the word with care. The dignity and quiet resolve that radiates from this modest woman who has triumphed over bone-deep ignorance and mindless brutality are profound.

Mukhtar Mai was raising funds for a co-ed high school for her village. After her story appeared in the New York Times in 2002, the Canadian consulate in the capital of Islamabad sent two people with a check for one hundred thousand dollars for her first grammar school, which she built. Education is everything to Mukhtar.

Once she decided not to commit suicide and fight for justice, she went to the police with her father. An officer took notes as she told of the attack. Mukhtar was illiterate, so when the police told her to give her approval by placing a thumbprint on the paper, she did. Mukhtar tells her audience this inability to read haunted her and, when the report was later proven to be a bold lie, convinced her that she and the village women and children must learn to read.

After being publicly kicked in the political shins by Condoleezza Rice over this case, Prime Minister General Musharraf provided Mukhtar with 24-hour armed protection. It's necessary because the Mostoi men have sworn to kill her. She tells us that she fully expects to die by their hands and is in a hurry to get the high school and a refuge for women built. She shelters five women in her tiny three-room house. Her home is within sight of the Mostoi compound. Presently, the armed protection is down to one man with a gun whom she must provide with meals.

Her now ten-year saga has taken remarkable twists and turns. In 2003, six men were given the death penalty and ordered to pay Mukhtar Rs.50,000 (about $790.00). Her attorney revealed at trial that the rape of Mukhtar was to cover the rape of her young brother in a field by several Mostoi men. Four were Mostoi, and two were from the village 'court' that ordered the rape. The rest of the clan members involved were set free. Since the Pakistani elections in January of 2008, Musharraf has lost power, and Mukhtar's protection is again in question.

There are many ironies in Mukhtar's story, but one of the most poignant is that several of her students are children of the men who violated her and gang-raped her younger brother. She is pleased they attend, she tells us, because she must "Fight injustice through knowledge and education."

Mukhtar Mai signed all the books that night with her full name. She can read and write at last and the following day flew home to Pakistan, where she is one of the teachers in her precious school.

On her three-city fundraising trip to America that December, Mukhtar raised over $168,000. Her new co-ed high school opened in March of 2009, with supporters from several countries attending. Now Mukhtar is working on the women's shelter.

I love this woman.

Mukhtar has expanded her role in the community to that of counselor and intermediary for abused women. She travels with two armed police officers and goes to abused women's homes to talk to and warn husbands about their behavior.

On April 10, 2010, Mukhtar accepted the repeated marriage proposal from the man who had been guarding her for the past several years. Pakistan allows up to four wives; he already has one wife and lives several miles away. Mukhtar's condition of marriage; he signs his present home over to his first wife and then allows Mukhtar to remain in her own house, close to her schools. He can visit her whenever he wishes. He agreed to all her points. They have since had a son and now have a non-profit benefiting women and children.

MukhtarMai.org

In 2011, Pakistan's Supreme Court overturned four of the five convictions, and four of her attackers were released. Her attorneys are appealing.

"Today India has the largest number of out-of-school children in the world and one of the world's largest reservoirs of trained and skilled manpower."

Pawan K. Varma, **Being Indian**

Brighter Than the Sun

There's an irrepressible light in a young child's eyes. Perhaps it's a combination of innocence, the joy of being alive, curiosity in all things, and the mix of that child's unique being. Some shine more brightly than others, and once in a great while, you meet one that outshines the sun.

My husband, Gopal, and I were driving by the underside of a mid-town overpass in Patiala, India, three winters ago. Our street ran parallel to the overpass road. Under the four-lane "fly over," there was a long stretch of dirt, and as the upper road came to ground level, old construction materials filled the ever-narrowing wedge. You could access this dirt area on either side. One enterprising tea seller had rolled his portable stand into the center, set up plastic tables and chairs, and voila, he had an outdoor restaurant. The rumble of traffic and the constant blast of horns above and on both sides were deafening.

There was a traffic jam ahead, causing our car to stop. Before the ceiling reached ground level, I looked at the area next to the last big support pillars. The surface at this end of the block was covered with sharp rocks the size of tennis balls. A woman was squatting by a large, torn plastic bag and rummaging through the contents.

Thin ropes strung between the pillars held ragged blankets in a vain attempt at privacy. Next to the mother stood a girl about three years old; she was looking at me and grinning with the pleasure of a shared secret. Her little hands were balled into fists that she held to her chest. We were in on something together, she'd decided. I waved, and she flapped her little hands with glee. She had me.

The next day we filled a bag with essential food items and added a big bunch of bananas at the last minute. In search of access, we turned down the quieter side of the dirt block and drove in between the tea tables and the blanket curtains. The girl was engrossed with something on the ground and didn't see us at first. Her mother, barely 90 pounds and old beyond her years, got up from a pile of filthy bedding and warily watched us walk to her. The surroundings were meager--heaps of tattered clothing, a cooking pot, but no sign of a coal burner or fire. Recycled plastic bottles held brown water carried from a source somewhere.

Then, the little girl looked up and saw us. Her face lit in excitement as she stood barefoot and started running the gauntlet of sharp rocks, nails, broken bottles, garbage, and scrap iron. Her mother watched with resignation and an awkward half smile. The child grew shy as she got to us and looked to Gopal for a signal.

I took out the bananas, tore off a bunch of three, and handed them to her. She squealed in delight and turned to show her mother this bonanza. "Bananas are her favorite," the mother told us. The child took my hand so readily that it brought tears to my eyes-- instant trust for a world that had done little to earn it so far.

Since the day before, when she had been dirty with matted hair and only a ragged blouse for cover, her mother had bathed her, and she now had fairly good clothes.

Her parents were from another state and spoke only broken Hindi, so Gopal had some difficulty learning their situation. The father (who arrived drunk but happy) was a rickshaw driver.

His face had a boyish sweetness, but life had also aged him too quickly. With red rheumy eyes, he kept by his rickshaw watching us with a drunk's occasional moment of clarity--the strangers had brought his family what he could not. His daughter was blissfully unaware and clapped with delight when her mother peeled a banana for her. She thrust it out to show us her prize, then thought better of it and ran to offer us a piece.

Her mother accepted the food bag but would wait until we left to find tea, rice, lentils, salt, sugar, oil, peanuts, soap, matches, and toffees to last a week. We came by two days later with more supplies and sandals for the girl and her mother but had to suspend our plans for the family until we returned from a three-day trip to Delhi.

It was urgent to get the girl immunized and then into pre-K at a nearby school before the parents sent her to beg in a year or two. If we could find a better shelter for them and the mother could have a semblance of a home, she might fight to stay put, and the child, perhaps, could remain in school and relatively safe.

As we waved goodbye to 'Sunshine,' Gopal took a picture of her holding her prized banana. We told her we would be back in three days. She held her little hand up with three fingers pointing out. I did the same, and she giggled with pride at our shared accomplishment.

As our car pulled away, she toddled along with us a few feet before stopping, and with one fist against her chest, she rocked to and fro with simple joy. That day I promised her and myself that we would do everything possible to keep her from the streets.

On the train early the following day, we read in the newspaper that a delegation from a Pakistani sports association would be visiting Patiala while we were gone. We mused over the love/hate relationship

Indians have with the Pakistanis and gave it no further thought.

On our first morning back, we put another food bag together with a big bunch of bananas for our girl and, with plans for school, set off early to see her and her mother. As we rounded the corner nearest their space, we were stunned to see that the entire block-long area under the flyover had been bulldozed, leveled, and cleared of all cars, tea sellers, debris, and the little family. The block had been enclosed with a heavy wrought iron fence to impress the Pakistanis who would drive down the street for three minutes.

The two eager young men who drove us that visit were dispatched to find Sunshine. A sizeable reward was promised as we clipped her picture to their sun visor. We went into dicey areas, showing her photo and describing her father, offering money if anyone could find her. We visited the rest stops for rickshaw drivers, but there are thousands of rickshaws in the city.

Gopal walked into tent camps along the railroad tracks where marihuana grows wild and might have attracted the father—but no one knew them. Weeks passed, and some shop owners near the flyover said the family would return. We searched until our last day but never found her. She's around six now and probably an accomplished beggar, her remarkable light flickering out, if not already gone. For one brief moment, she was incandescent with promise and joy, and we will never forget her.

Sunshine at home under the flyover

"Few fathers care much for their sons, or at least, most of them care more for their money. Of those who really love their sons, few know how to do it."

Lord Chesterfield

The Sharpest Sting

In Agra, India, there lived a wealthy man with a wife and two sons. Friends and family enjoyed pointing out the obvious; he was doubly blessed in a country that prizes sons over daughters.

One year apart, the boys were denied nothing from the moment they were born. In a culture where parents rarely discipline their young children, the boys were allowed to terrorize their cousins and playmates with impunity. Their mother tried to correct the boys, but the father always intervened. As they entered their teens, they spent more and more time with their indulgent father.

For the boys' eighteenth birthdays, they were each given a German sports car with a trip to Germany to choose the model. Their father glowed with pride and love and could not remember his life before his sons were born.

Dismayed at her husband's indulgence and the boorish behavior of her boys, his wife longed for a daughter to cherish, but it was not to be. She hid her disappointment and, over the years, found solace in her books. She was especially fond of Shakespeare.

One day, she instructed the chauffeur to drive her to the marble artisan's shop. There was a story that his ancestors had worked on the Taj Mahal. Whatever the truth, he was the best in the city.

She chose a small slab of polished, pink marble and told him the words to inscribe. When she brought it home, she placed it with her favorite books on the shelf. Her husband took no notice.

The patriarch next door relished reminding the father of his good fortune.

"The time will come when you can no longer do for yourself. Your boys will then care for you until your last breath, as my son now cares for me. Your daughters-in-law will prepare your favorite dishes, your grandchildren will amuse you, and your family will attend to every whim. This is a great life, and you have been doubly blessed."

The father agreed and thought briefly of one cousin who had moved to Canada years before. The poor man had no servants, worked all week in his office, and spent weekends working in his yard and attending his children's sports activities—what a strange life.

When the rich man's eldest son entered a prestigious university, the father decided it was time to build a larger house. His wife disagreed. Their home was more than suitable for two future daughters-in-law, she argued. Could he not see he was spoiling their boys? Nonsense. The father was adamant, and besides, what did she know of such matters? Nothing was too good for his sons.

Weary, his wife retreated to her study and her books. She would gaze at the words carved in pink marble and become lost in thought.

For a college graduation present, the father presented his firstborn with the newly completed and furnished second floor, ten spacious rooms with a modern kitchen and a servants' wing. The son pointed out that the servants' quarters were rather small. He preferred the ground floor, but he would bide his time, as everything would come to him eventually. Soon he joined his father's business as a senior executive.

The second son graduated one year later and, like his brother, joined his father's business. He now owned the third floor, ten large rooms with a modern kitchen and servants' wing. However, he complained that his brother's second-floor balcony had a better view of the park.

Inevitably talk of marriage began for the boys. Their mother did her duty and found two suitable girls from good families for the brothers.

It was decided that a double wedding would be

held. The lavish ceremony and reception, with no extravagance overlooked, did justice to the family's wealth. Toasts to the parents' good fortunes were too numerous to count.

Then tragedy struck. When the couples returned from their honeymoons, they learned that the boys' mother had suddenly passed away. Her friends whispered that she had died from deep loneliness, but the family took no heed.

After an elaborate funeral, it was their people's custom to give family and friends items that were held dear by their mother. When almost everything was gone, the husband entered her study, and it was then that he saw the pink marble so beautifully inscribed for the first time.

The father now had the entire ground floor to himself and his four servants. His beloved sons and their wives settled into their homes upstairs and, after the first weeks of having their meals together, found it a nuisance to come down so often to keep their father company.

They presented him with a proposal. On alternate days he would come upstairs and have his meals with one of the couples. This worked out to fifteen days a month with each son. The first day's meals would be taken with his eldest, the second with his youngest, and so on. To console himself, the father reasoned, *my boys are very busy, so perhaps this is better all around.*

It so happened that this proposal was made in January. On the thirty-first day, he arrived for breakfast at the flat of his elder son.

He was stopped at the door.

"Sorry, but we've done fifteen days already; you must go upstairs."

Taken aback, the father trudged up the stairs and knocked. He was stunned to hear the exact words come from his youngest boy's lips, "We've done our fifteen days."

As he slowly shuffled down the two flights of stairs, he pressed his hand against his chest, holding in a heart grown too heavy to bear.

He stopped going to his sons' flats for meals and became busy with other matters. He began using his wife's study, and while going over his papers late into the night, he would unconsciously caress the cool marble that he now kept near.

One evening, just before dinner, the elder son came to see his father about an errant servant. He was shocked when a strange man met him at the door. Beyond him, he could see a family sitting at his parents' dining table.

"Who are you?" the son demanded.

"I'm the new owner of this house and your father's business," the man replied.

He added, smiling, "You've saved me a trip upstairs. You and your brother are terminated. You have fifteen days to vacate your offices and homes, which shouldn't be a problem. I'm told you're both experts at counting to fifteen."

Rumor had it that the father was living in Canada though no one knew for sure. It was said the only keepsake he took from the house was a piece of pink marble inscribed with words expressed more than 400 years before by another grieving father:

"Sharper than a serpent's tooth is the sting of an ungrateful child."
King Lear, *William Shakespeare*

"Every child you encounter is a divine appointment."

Wes Stafford

In a Field of Marigolds

Northern India

January wind whistled through the orphanage's broken windowpanes as forty-two girls burrowed deeper under their patched quilts. Six of the smallest slept two to a cot and held tight in sleep. Kiran, the eldest at 18, pulled the quilt down to peek at the clock on her locker; 6 a.m. glowed in green. Lovely, the youngest orphan at two years old, snuggled against her and slept on.

Matron Aunty would come soon to wake the girls. Management expected Kiran to supervise the dressing and washing of faces, combing hair, tying ribbons, snapping barrettes, gathering books, and trooping downstairs to breakfast.

Then she remembered today was Sunday. No school. Even better, Neeta, the second oldest at 17, was getting married. Local snack shops would bring hot, flaky samosas, potato cutlets, sweets, and continuous hot tea. The remaining forty-one girls would dig out their donated party dresses and shoes, and they all knew lipstick and jewelry were allowed for weddings. Everyone would be giddy with excitement, chattering and laughing as they admired each other's outfits.

For a few hours, they would forget they were orphans.

After several years, the younger girls' memories of their previous lives would all but fade. This cold, broken-down building would be home for the rest of their childhood until the orphanage board, led by the elderly manager, Mrs. Seth, would find a succession of boys on the fringes of respectable society and marry the girls off, one by one.

Neeta, the soon-to-be bride, slept soundly, unconcerned by the pending life change. Two months ago, she'd been allowed to view the boy she was to marry from across the visiting room where he sat with his mother, forlorn as a sacrificial goat. Casting furtive glances her way, he finally settled his eyes on his hands, resigned to his fate.

Two orphanage board members acting as Neeta's parents and the boy's mother and uncle signed the marriage contract. Neeta would bring her in-laws a modest but respectable dowry supplied to every bride by doner supporters of the orphanage. There would be two sets of jewelry, six saris, six shalwar kameez outfits, one suit for the groom, complete outfitting for a small kitchen, two new blankets with sheets, a cell phone, and a new bicycle. The groom's family promised to provide the couple a bedroom and treat Neeta as a family member, not a servant. As custom dictated, nothing was asked of the young couple.

Neeta was placidly accepting of Mrs. Seth's choice. He had two arms and two legs, was free of any visible disease, appeared sane, and had a job—the essential requirements. Whether he was of good character, had a sense of humor, or was kind to animals was of no consequence to anyone.

Unlike many orphans, Kiran had painful, vivid memories of sitting around the table with her Sikh parents and two younger sisters late at night, having their customary bedtime tea together before her mom tucked the girls in.

"Hug me goodnight, Mommy," she remembered asking before the pounding on the front door began.

"Who could that be this late?" her mother asked before they heard the door crash, her father protesting, scuffling, teacups crashing to the stone floor.

Then, the wrenching desperation in his voice when he shouted, "Take the girls --- run!"

Mother and daughters bolted from the back door as gunfire and the security of their lives exploded behind them.

It was 1986, and the revenge killing of Sikhs for Indira Gandhi's assassination by her Sikh bodyguard had spread across Punjab. Kiran, her mother, and sisters watched from a neighbor's window as thugs doused their house in gasoline. Their mother, insane with shock and screaming her husband's name, ran from their side into the flames.

Fearing for their own lives, the neighbors pushed the terrified girls out into the night and locked their doors. Kiran, barely eleven, led her sisters to a dry ditch where they huddled for two days, frozen in fear. When police finally arrived to inspect the fire, she ran to the only officer wearing a familiar Sikh turban, and they were quickly deposited at the orphanage.

Six days later, when word had traveled through the family grapevine, their mother's older sister arrived. After inspecting her three nieces and giving them all pats on their heads, she hurried to the manager's office to complete her familial task before catching the last train back to Delhi.

Mrs. Seth summoned Kiran and her sisters. Their aunt would take the two youngest girls, five and seven, and perhaps if her fortunes improved, she would return for Kiran in the future. For the second time in eight days, the sisters were grief-stricken and clung to each other before Mrs. Seth pulled the little ones away. Girls eventually require dowries, making them a financial burden, and this aunt already had a girl of her own.

In Amritsar, Kiran's married cousin, Sheila, wrote to her regularly. Twice after she entered her teens,

Mrs. Seth allowed her to visit Sheila, a teacher, during the summer school break. Only Sheila knew that Kiran had met a young man, Dev, on her first visit. One summer, when she was seventeen, Dev led her to a field of marigolds, where they lay hidden from the world.

Dev's warm eyes and calm voice soothed her aching heart. He'd gathered a handful of marigold petals and laid them in a pattern on Kiran's skin. "One day, I will place our wedding garlands around your neck, and you will garland me as your groom. We are engaged as of this day." She remembered praying, *God bless our happiness and hold our joy to your heart.*

Pledging one's love is no small feat in a culture that forbids love marriages; that will exile children who insist on choosing whom they marry; a culture that has looked the other way when daughters are killed for marrying on their own. Even without the benefit of a family, every girl knew the orphanage management would enforce the rules.

More than most children, Kiran understood how tenuous life was and how a knock on the door can destroy everything you hold dear. She had already caused grumbling among the board members for refusing their first suggestion that she was ready to marry. They had moved on to Neeta, but she was next, and they would not tolerate another refusal.

Today, she would enjoy the festivities. About thirty families supported the orphanage with annual pledges and gifts for the dowries. Twice in recent years, a wealthy person gave a lump sum for new chairs or fans for the rooms. Items the managers were glad to buy and display. Fixing broken windows, buying blankets, or putting in hot water tanks were never options. Mrs. Seth repeatedly said, "It's only cold four months out of the year."

The girls rushed down the narrow stairs and raced each other to the cafeteria. They grabbed their metal trays and lined up for hot porridge. There was little complaining, for there would be more than enough to eat in a few hours.

The spicy fragrance of marigolds that always heralded a wedding flooded the courtyard. Garland makers carried in dozens of gold and orange strands for the ceremony. Kiran breathed in deeply and closed her eyes, *soon, my love.*

On marriage days, the management put on its best face. This was a promising opportunity to woo new supporters and show families with sons that the orphanage girls weren't so bad. Being around orphans risked bad karma—their misfortunes could rub off if you got too close. Donations were given, but don't touch the "inmates."

Only naïve foreigners ever sat down and talked with the girls, got to know, and gave them desperately needed hugs. Only bothersome westerners pointed out that criminals were called inmates; these children were innocent victims, and this cold stone building was their home.

Kiran smiled as she dressed with extra care; her plan was almost ready. Cousin Sheila was coming today and would mingle with the other guests. She'll say she came to visit Kiran and didn't realize there was a marriage. Then, while Mrs. Seth is flush with the success of the wedding, Sheila will casually suggest that she knows of a good, suitable boy for Kiran, and perhaps they can talk about it in a few weeks.

Everyone knows the managers strongly prefer finding the boy themselves. Total control until the end — and they will be suspicious. But they always have trouble finding good prospects, so perhaps they will be relieved this one time. Kiran forgoes the allowed makeup for the occasion. No point in risking offending the older conservatives on the board.

The girls shrieked from the cold water as they washed their hair quickly in the freezing washrooms. The sun had yet to break through the clouds, and Kiran gritted her teeth in anger. The manager and matron sat downstairs in cozy comfort, sipping their hot tea, tucked around two big room heaters, while the children upstairs were denied even hair dryers.

Suddenly, Kiran heard her name called by Matron Aunty. "You're wanted in the office." Kiran grabbed her shawl and hurried downstairs, wondering what had happened now.

Seth, and another board member, Mrs. Jhalawar, were sitting in the visitor's room with their arms crossed against the cold. Mrs. Jhalawar, mean and spiteful, gave money to the orphanage, so she was allowed to poke her nose into every girl's business. Kiran's heart sank when she saw a familiar blue envelope in Mrs. Seth's hand, the last letter from cousin Sheila. Someone had found it under her cot and passed it to the matron, who dutifully gave it to Manager Seth. Kiran tried to scramble a defense before the manager, waving the letter like a small flag of triumph, spoke.

"Girl, what do you think? We are all stupid here and don't know about your boyfriend in Amritsar. You have disgraced our organization after all we've done for you. We would never find suitable grooms if word got out that our girls may *know* boys."

Deciding the only defense was to bow her head and appear contrite, Kiran remained silent as Mrs. Jhalawar warmed to the task. "You miserable little tramp! Sneaking behind our backs, kissing, and worse, I'm sure...."

But Kiran could not bear this accusation. "No, you're wrong, I'm chaste and good, and we've only held hands—nothing more. Dev is a decent boy; you cannot accuse us; you know nothing!"

Mrs. Jhalawar smirked in sly triumph. She'd tricked Kiran into admitting she had a boyfriend and even supplied his name. Any physical contact was lumped into one big sin. *Oh god, how stupid, how stupid*, Kiran berated herself, but the damage was done. They would lock her down and marry her to some tea stall owner with rotting teeth within the month.

"Get back to the girls and see they are dressed and ready. Guests will arrive at noon, and we will deal with you this evening."

Mrs. Seth liked Kiran and admired her maturity and poise. This discovery was a blow to her judgment, and she was livid.

The wedding distracted management and the board members and allowed Kiran to keep a vigil near the gate until she saw her cousin arrive. Rushing to Sheila, she sobbed, "They know everything and will have me married within weeks. Please, tell Dev I'm leaving this evil place and coming to him."

But it wasn't that simple. Years earlier, having signed Kiran over to the orphanage, her aunt was made free of financial responsibilities but lost all control of Kiran's future. By law, she belonged to the managers until she turned nineteen.

Unaware of these legal strings, two nights later, while the night watchman dozed on his cot near the gate, Kiran slipped out and made her way to the bus station five blocks away. She caught the midnight bus to Amritsar and was met four hours later by Dev, cousin Sheila, and her husband.

Mrs. Seth, desperate to head off any bad publicity, called the Amritsar Police and reported her missing. The police, with addresses and names, quickly found Kiran and returned her to the orphanage, plunging her and most of the girls into a deep depression. The older girls had been hanging on every detail of Kiran's romance and were secretly thrilled when she made it to Dev. Bollywood movies couldn't compete with this romantic and exciting storyline.

Days, then weeks went by with letters to Dev smuggled out by sympathetic visitors, and occasionally, one from him would make its way inside.

One morning, Mrs. Jhalawar announced that she had a nephew who would marry Kiran, and he was only 36 years old. Kiran stopped eating, and in sympathy, five of the older girls joined her hunger strike, sending the board into near panic. On the seventh day, a doctor was called.

Word of the hunger strike reached cousin Sheila. Two days later, she arrived late afternoon, gambling that, like most elderly Indians, Mrs. Seth took a nap after lunch, leaving only a matron in charge.

Having paid a small bribe in Amritsar, Sheila now produced an official-looking paper with ink barely dry and placed it on the desk. Matron Aunty, illiterate but with dignity, pretended to read the document nodding here and there as she came to the bottom of the page.

Fully aware the older woman did not know the meaning, Sheila said, "So, we agree, I will help Kiran pack," and walked out of the office and up the stairs to the girls' quarters.

The two cousins came down in less than eight minutes with one small suitcase. The girls, sisters in spirit for the past seven years, followed her gleefully to the gate. The youngest, Lovely, rescued as a discarded newborn, looked to Kiran as a mother and clung to her legs, begging her to stay. Seema, now the oldest and the new leader, picked Lovely up as the torch was gently passed, and Kiran hugged them all farewell.

As Kiran left the orphanage and the neighborhood in her cousin's car, her elation was mixed with sadness. Her sisters were far away, growing up without her. She promised her parents' spirit that she would do everything she could to bring them to Amritsar to live.

When Mrs. Seth returned soon after, she warily studied the document. It was Kiran's new and revised birth certificate, declaring that on this day, she turned nineteen. Everyone's face was saved, and the manager reluctantly conceded defeat.

Two weeks later, Kiran and Dev married in Amritsar with garlands of marigolds and with love in the room not seen perhaps since Shah Jahan, for his beloved Mumtaz 400 years before, created an exquisite and timeless memorial, the Taj Mahal.

Kiran and Dev have a daughter, fourteen, and a son, eight. With a prickly truce in place, she and her husband attend every wedding at the orphanage, invited or not. Her younger sisters joined her and Dev two years later. She continues to assure us that one day her children will decide whom they marry.

After ten months, a joyous reunion with the girls

"There are only two ways to live your life. One is as though nothing is a miracle.
The other is as though everything is a miracle."

Albert Einstein

All Is Well

Ten-year-old Sadhu sat on the step of his one-room house and watched school children in their blue uniforms head home laughing and eating lunch leftovers. One of the boys tossed an apple over his shoulder. As the students turned the corner, Sadhu raced to the gutter and grabbed the prize. Two of India's feral dogs trotted over to see if he'd found anything worth fighting for, but the apple held no interest.

Down the lane was the two-room house of his grown-up friend, Naresh. Sadhu scurried up the side stairs to his friend's flat roof, where he could eat in peace. He bit into his apple—worm-eaten. Carefully he picked out the worm parts and ate everything but the bitter seeds. Needing someone to talk to, he was tempted to knock on Naresh's door, but his friend had a night job and slept during the day.

Sadhu walked to the produce sellers in search of discarded vegetables. His mother would start their one meal soon. The brown lentil, a staple of the poor, was 120 rupees a kilo. On a good night of fetching and carrying at weddings and festivals, Sadhu could make 20 or 30 rupees. The gamble was getting paid. At the end of work, when the head runner divided the wages, he was usually ignored.

Near the fruit stands, he noticed agitated people and two police officers passing out flyers. Sadhu sidled up, hoping to hear the heated discussion. He couldn't read and yearned for school, but it was beyond his mother's meager income. The uniform and books were over 700 rupees.

People from the better neighborhoods came to this outdoor market to buy their produce. "It's an outrage!" said one man as he shook the flyer and looked around for an audience. "We're not safe in our own homes."

A woman wrapped in Pashmina agreed, "What are we paying the *chowkidar* for? Isn't he supposed to spot trouble and alert the police?"

The chowkidar, or night watchman, was a centuries-old tradition still essential to Indian life. Households in a mile-square neighborhood paid a fee for a man carrying a long lathi, or pole, to walk their streets. Every few houses, he would hit the ground with the pole and call out, *"Jagte raho, sabh theek hai"* "Be awake, all is well!" Homeowners would hear the knock of the steel tip, and the reassuring call repeated for blocks as they drifted off to sleep.

Sadhu meandered through the crowd gathering details as people were more than willing to spread bad news.

"They robbed the Patels of their silver and rupees while they slept. And that's not all. The widow Singh, alone and defenseless in the next lane, didn't hear a sound. Most of her gold, right out of her closet next to her bed—gone!"

Sadhu's mother, Neena, cleaned house for the widow Singh who cheated Neena in pay more times than not. Most big houses cheated the poor, who were often illiterate but not stupid, though this distinction was seldom made.

When news of the robberies spread from big houses to mini-mansions, suspicions quickly fell upon the servants. Fingers were pointed at maids, cooks, and *ayahs* (nannies). Soon the finger was pointed at Neena, and a young policeman arrived to search their modest home. When the last of their rice, barely a cup, was tossed onto the dirt floor by the cop, Sadhu grabbed the flour sack and ran before their only remaining food was destroyed.

The smirking policeman suggested Neena could be friendlier and maybe he would take her name off the list, but a curious neighbor asked if everything was okay, and he left in a huff. It took an hour for mother and son to pick up every grain of rice. A half-rotten potato and a few leaves of scavenged cabbage made their supper that night.

Wild rumors continued racing through the neighborhoods, leaving rich and poor on edge. Only the impending arrival of Diwali, India's biggest holiday, took everyone's mind off their troubles. The nightly call of the chowkidar that all was well reminded the homeowners that something was still right in the universe.

One more house was robbed, the police chief's no less, but the family had been away, taking their guard dog with them. Poetic justice said the poor, and others called it karma.

Servants were always overworked on Diwali Eve. Guests stopping by expected tea and hot snacks, and the big dinners required endless runs to the market for supplies. The servants felt exploited like no other time of year. Extra pay was unheard of, as was a day off. Help worked seven days a week, with only a servant's family wedding, the sacrosanct event, worthy of missed work. Every servant knew wedding was the word that got them a day off.

Something was abuzz in the servant community, and by noon on Diwali Eve, maids, cooks, sweepers, and nannies had told dozens of big homeowners that there was a last-minute wedding to attend. No amount of cajoling could sway their decision to miss work on the busy holiday. Threats were tossed around, with two or three faces slapped for good measure, but the homeowners were helpless.

Neena and Sadhu warmed a bucket of water over the kerosene burner, and each took a bath with their sliver of sandalwood soap. Neena laid out their best clothes, thread-bare and reserved for only the most special occasion, which this night promised to be.

While his mother finished dressing, Sadhu looked at their beautiful party invitation sent to everyone in the servant community like a miracle the week before. He could recognize his name at the top. A drawing of the moon and stars said a night event, and the water tower told him just where in town they were going. Though it was a party and not a wedding, the servant grapevine had unanimously agreed—the word was, they were all attending a wedding.

Somehow, his mother had found a few coins for a bicycle rickshaw. Sadhu would not worry; he and his mother must enjoy every second of the magical night. As the rickshaw carried them along, his mother relaxed and began smiling.

"Look, darling, at all the Diwali lights, aren't they lovely, how gay!" Every house was outlined in fairy lights; some blinked, others twinkled, and a few homes chose the old-fashioned oil lamps carefully spaced on the roofline. It was wondrous.

A vaguely familiar man greeted people at the party tent's entrance and handed each guest a gold box tied with a red silk ribbon. He wore a fancy Indian suit of white Jodhpur pants under a long red coat covered in gold embroidery. The tent shimmered in tiny lights, and there were large bouquets of roses and jasmine on every table. The guests were in awe and waited patiently in line.

Sadhu had worked enough parties to know how costly just the decorations were. Who was their host? He recognized a servant boy in line from the police chief's house, who bounced up and down with excitement as tears of joy rolled down his cheeks.

At last, their turn came. "Welcome, friends. Happy Diwali!" Sadhu's mouth fell open. Naresh, his friend three doors down wearing a silk turban, grabbed his hand and shook it, then greeted his mother, Neena. "Come in, come in and eat and dance the night away with your friends. This is our party!"

In a daze, Neena led her son into the tent. Over a hundred people were laughing, eating, and dancing. The gold boxes clutched in their hands were heavy. "Let's sit down, Mother. I want to open our gifts."

Neena handed her box to Sadhu. "You open them, darling. I just saw my friend who cooks for widow Singh." Neena patted his cheek, then hurried off, bubbly with excitement.

Sadhu untied the beautiful silk ribbons and carefully rolled up each length, tucking them into his pocket before lifting the lids. For his mother, a large stack of paper money and a gold necklace with earrings lay shimmering in red tissue. In his larger box were 1000 rupees in a silk bag, a fortune for their empty coffers. Then, neatly folded, a blue and gray school uniform and a pair of shoes lay under a layer of red tissue.

The DJ stopped the Bollywood music as Naresh asked everyone to take a seat because dinner was ready. Neena found Sadhu and led him to a table of friends. There were the cook and the sweeper for the police station with his frail wife. Next to them was the young servant girl from the Patel house who had been slapped just yesterday. None had ever been served at a table. They ate their meals while squatting on the floors of their employers' kitchens.

Naresh had hired a catering company to cook and serve the guests. Sadhu recognized one waiter who had cheated him of pay more than once. His head spun as he felt his world tilt.

Then, the food came. The mouth-watering fragrance of hot *ghee,* clarified butter, the mark of no cost spared, wafted over the tables. Flaky bread, fresh from the tandoori ovens, succulent basmati rice rich in cashews and raisins, then covered in edible silver leaf, came in waves from the chefs.

Those who preferred meat had lamb worthy of the Moguls, the plumpest game hens, and wild boar soaked in pomegranate juice and then roasted in beds of charcoal for an entire day—the feasting went on for hours.

Silk pillows lined the tent so guests could lie down and digest for a while before returning to the tables for the platters of dates, nuts, sweetmeats, and all the hot tea they could drink. People called out for their favorite movie songs and danced around the tent. Everyone could, at last, laugh and eat their fill. The elderly, in service since childhood, held each other, shaking their heads in disbelief.

Naresh took the microphone and thanked everyone for coming.

"My friends, this evening is long overdue, and every person here deserves this night and much more. The gifts of money are for your children's education. Promise me you would send the children to school for only they will care for you in later years. They are the future."

The people shouted and applauded, "Yes, you are right!"

Sadhu hugged his uniform to his chest and looked up at his mother with such yearning, her eyes filled with tears. Then, smiling, Naresh glanced at Sadhu and told a story as the beer began to flow.

"There was a poor factory worker who pushed his wheelbarrow out the gate every day at quitting time. The guard would carefully search the wheelbarrow for contraband and then wave the worker through. After 35 years, when the poor worker retired to a villa by the sea, the guard called him up and asked how he'd done it because he, the guard, had so carefully checked each day. 'What were you stealing?' The worker replied, 'Wheelbarrows.'"

As the people roared with laughter, others became emboldened and took the microphone to tell their stories of the cleverness and stupidity of man. Finally, with every drop drunk and every grain of rice consumed, it was time to go home. The guests gathered their gifts and searched for their host to no avail. Well, no matter, they would find him tomorrow and give him their thanks.

Something was bouncing around in Sadhu's thoughts. That wheelbarrow story and the look from Naresh. With the three-house advantage, Sadhu ran to his friend's door, eager to thank him. But his knock went unanswered. Frustrated, he hurried up the stairs to the roof where his friend sometimes slept. Nothing but Naresh's old bike and a lathi lay on the floor. Sadhu started down the stairs and then stopped.

He looked at the lathi, then picked up one end. The pole was hollow, and something inside slid down and landed on his toe. He searched in the faint light of the Diwali lights and found a small gold earring. Sadhu turned to the bike and saw a flat metal box taped to the handlebars; it had buttons and a lever that he pushed. A voice cried out, startling the boy. It was Naresh calling, "Be awake, all is well," followed by a thwack that Sadhu recognized as the lathi hitting the ground. The voice and thwacks repeated, fading to the end. Sadhu sat down with a thud. He pulled the silk ribbons from his pocket, studied the gold earring, and began to laugh

Chowkidar, night watchman on duty

"Don't leave the decision of who you are going to be in the hands of others. That power was given to you alone."

Jennifer Kirklin

Labeling Kristen

"Dad, I'm not going. Don't you and Mom get it? Not going! Not going! Not going!"

Kristen threw her ticket into the air and stomped out of the kitchen, sending the gold "Juicy" on her vintage baby blue pants into spastic jerks and bobbles. Her bedroom door slammed as Black Eyed Peas' greatest hits blasted through the walls.

"She is going, and she better get used to it. The world does not revolve around Kristen," said her father.

"Jim, shouldn't we take her to a therapist and let her vent with a third party? After all–," Kristen's mother responded.

"Oh, for Pete's sake, Liz. We're the parents, and she's the child, a spoiled, self-centered kid who needs to wake up and smell reality. Visiting Sri Lanka is the trip of a lifetime. Six weeks away from texting on that cell phone that's fused to her hand—that's therapy. She's fifteen and hasn't got a clue about the world. I doubt if she could find Europe on the map of Europe.

Our deadline is Sri Lanka by June 23 for the plant opening, but we can stop in Mumbai first, take the Bollywood tour, and spend a few days at the Oberoi Hotel on the beach. After that, it's goodbye luxury, hello reality." Jim did finger quotes and smiled sourly at his wit.

Liz had doubts that her fragile Little Miss Denver, and Colorado Junior Miss third runner-up Kristen, who could not stand an enriched hair out of place, would be able to take the heat and inconveniences looming on the near horizon. Liz had heard that some of Jim's colleagues in Colombo had to endure frequent power outages, no central air-conditioning, and finding Diet Coke was practically impossible.

Ten days later, their connecting flight from London was in its last two hours as Kristen studied her face in her oversized YSL make-up mirror.

"Mom, my Evian's empty, my eyes are puffy, and I look horrid; I'm not getting off the plane—forget it." Liz was looking at Jim for help when a triple bell tone announced the captain's voice.

"Ah, folks, we're being diverted to Ahmedabad due to a vehicle accident on the runway in Mumbai. Since air traffic is backed up and your connecting flights are also delayed, Virgin Atlantic wants to assure our passengers we will host you at hotels near the airport, and we apologize for this inconvenience. Virgin's ground personnel will give you the details as soon as we deplane. Ah, thanks for your understanding."

The look of horror on their daughter's face was almost comical, but Jim knew not to laugh. Major pouting with teen outrage would ensue, and he was too tired to deal with it.

"Hey, I always wanted to see Ahmedabad. This could be fun."

Kristen stared at her father as though he had sprouted a second nose. She threw her head onto the seatback, carefully adjusted her hot pink Ray-Bans, and began Olympic-level whining as their plane came in for the approach.

"Eeeww, what's that smell?" Their daughter had taken two steps off the plane before India's unique blend of smoke, fuel, spices, and cleaning fluids had reached inside the sealed jet-way. Her parents ignored her remark, but the Indian ground personnel heard her. The moving crowd of tired, anxious passengers pushed the family into the gate area and then to a harried, turbaned Virgin manager holding a list of hotels.

Twenty minutes later, Jim and Liz learned they would stay at the Oh Boy Roy Inn, a cheeky name rip-off of the famous and elegant Oberoi Hotel chain. Jim knew that a Kristen meltdown might be in the making, so he said nothing and took the three vouchers with resigned grace as the weary travelers continued to their next task.

"Indian customs officials do not flirt, banter, or joke," Jim warned, knowing Kristen had honed these skills to perfection on the beauty pageant circuit. "Just keep quiet and speak only when they ask you a question--are we clear?"

Her dad was dead serious, so Kristen answered with a pouty, "Yes," getting in one last eye roll and chest heave.

The stars were aligned for cosmic fun as Kristen's new YSL Kalahari Sand luggage was chosen for inspection.

"Please stand here and remove your sunglasses," the female customs agent instructed, indicating a yellow line in front of a long table. She took in Kristen's hair and expensive clothes as she slowly unzipped the designer bag, recognizing it as the real thing for a change.

The veteran pageant winner was about to say, "Isn't my new luggage color bitchin'?" but caught herself in time. Agent Singh lifted stacks of clothing and noted that every item in the suitcase had a designer label. Even the casual clothes shouted "Old Navy" and "Calvin" in bold print, and nothing looked worn. The customs agent was bored; the day had been slow, so *why not have a little fun*?

"Is your nickname Juicy? Do you forget who you are, and that's why you have your name on your bum? Is this old person, Navy, your grandfather? Does this Calvin also forget who he is?" Kristen looked around for her parents, who were busy at another table.

"Umm, no, those are the designer names. You know, the de-sign-ers."

Agent Singh unzipped a mint green bag with numerous tiny bottles, pencils, brushes, and small pots of cream. "You're an artist, a painter?"

"No, that's my beauty regimen," Kristen answered, bewildered.

"Your beauty what?" The woman looked at this odd child with pity.

"Are these made by your designers?" Agent Singh held up two pairs of Manolo Blahnik heels and a Coach bag.

"Yes, those are my favorite shoes and purse." Kristen felt her center shifting and sliding.

"Do the designers pay you to wear their names?" Agent Singh patted a big stack of tops and several cloth bags of shoes and purses while affecting a look of wide-eyed amazement.

"No, not at all." Kristen could not read this woman. She knew she was being assessed and evaluated, but her gut said her judge-watching skills wouldn't apply here.

"Oh, then you are friends with Mr. Manolo and Mr. Coach, is that it? These were gifts?"

"No, my parents bought them for me to wear."

"Of course, you pay them, now I see. And how much would these shoes, this bag, and these Lululemon sets cost in U.S. currency?"

"I..., let me think..., they would be about two thousand dollars, I guess."

"Two thousand dollars. And this piece of luggage?" Agent Singh's tone had changed, and Kristen, uneasy, felt she was now being chastised.

"The luggage, I'm not sure. You'll have to ask my dad."

But the experienced woman had no need; she knew an authentic YSL suitcase went for over $2,800.

"Enjoy your stay in India, Mr. and Mrs. Rivers." Jim and Liz were handed their documents before turning towards Kristen as Agent Singh finally stamped the custom clearance.

They pushed open the outside doors with their luggage cart, and the humid heat hit them like a giant steaming pillow. Even Jim, familiar with India's summers, gasped and braced himself for Kristen's standard whine, but she was quiet for once.

A Virgin Atlantic mini bus driver quickly loaded the family's and other passengers' bags and inched the bus through the lock of vehicles that forever circle and choke India's airports. Kristen stared at the people only inches from her in the nearest cars as the drivers expertly came within a hair's breadth of collision.

Finally, they arrived at the Oh Boy Roy Inn, and Jim's heart sank. The place would not make even a three-star category. But, it was only one night, he sighed, they would survive, and he didn't want Liz or Kristen to see he was upset.

Five adorable little girls, barefoot with plastic bracelets and black kohl around their big eyes, stood by the entrance watching the family unload. In a white, majordomo suit covered in gold braid and tassels that any Ritz Carlton would deem over the top, the doorman shooed the girls like a litter of puppies.

Kristen watched as they obediently scattered and re-grouped 20 feet away, holding their little hands out to each other until all were linked. They smiled shyly, and Kristen gave them a tiny wave, delighting her when they waved back and giggled. *Gosh, they are cute!*

Jim glanced at his daughter at that moment and was struck by the simple pleasure on her face. It was a rare moment to see Kristen free of the pose and attitude of general disdain that she and her friends wore as a badge of honor.

Leading his wife and daughter to the lobby, Jim suggested, "Let's go wash up and rest, then we'll have dinner and get to sleep for our plane at 8 a.m."

Two hours later, as they sat looking down at plates of food that bore little resemblance to anything familiar, Kristen asked if she could have an omelet.

"Nothing doing, kiddo. You agreed to at least try Indian food. Come on, this is chicken tikka, and that's spinach with little cheese crumbles. It's delicious. Give it a try."

Kristen had to admit the *naan* bread did smell enticing. Using a piece as a little scoop, she took a bite of the creamed spinach and chicken. A festival of flavors danced the rumba in her mouth. "Mmm, this is super good; order more naan, okay?"

"Look at that, Liz, just like Jack Sprat, she licked her platter clean!"

"Well, it was excellent, and the mango ice cream was yummy."

Their daughter used "yummy" only when she was completely relaxed and herself. Risking the usual rejection, Liz reached over and squeezed her girl's hand, and Kristen surprised her mom by pressing back with a quick smile.

As they crossed the small lobby entrance to the stairs, Kristen looked out the double doors and saw the little girls on the driveway. It hit her then; *they're begging.*

In her 15.5 years of dance classes, birthday parties, pageants, and football rallies, Kristen had never seen a desperately hungry child. She knew they were out there, somewhere in cyberspace, because pictures popped up occasionally on her computer and television screen. *For only 79 cents a day, you can help a child like Maria.* But this was real, here, now, and it shook Kristen from her Ray Bans nestled in her $300 streaked-with-amber-highlights hair to her platform Jimmy Choos.

"Dad, is it okay if I stay and have an iced coffee? I'm not at all sleepy?"

Liz and Jim looked at each other--how nice and rather weird. Their daughter asked politely for a change, and they could see no real reason to say no.

"Okay, just sign for the drink on our room tab, and try to come up in an hour."

Kristen completed her parent's surreal evening by kissing each one on the cheek before returning to the dining room. Thirty minutes later, there was rapid knocking on their door, and the night manager, Mr. Ghoshswami, was nod-shaking his head and wringing his hands in distress.

"Mr. Rivers, excuse please this rudest and untimely intrusion into your much deserved rest from such a long and exhausting trip, isn't it..."

"What's the problem, Mr. Ghoshswami?"

"So kindly, please, sir, would you follow to the dining room?" His head bobbled as he held his hand out, sweeping *this way*.

"Let's go and get it over with, Liz; must be a misunderstanding with the bill."

As her parents entered the dining room, Kristen looked up. Jim would later tell his sister in Colorado that his daughter's face was radiant with a kind of bliss. Every one of the 15 chairs held a street child, and every child was intently slurping down a bowl of mango ice cream. Kristen cradled a ragamuffin toddler on her lap, tenderly spooning ice cream into an eager rosebud mouth.

"Sir, Mr. Rivers, sir, please only I'm asking, this is allowed by you? Mine is respectable inn; your daughter has brought in, how can I say, ah, ah, these—"

"Our daughter has brought in hungry children, Mr.

Ghoshswami, and you sell food. Whatever they want, let them have."

"Dad, about the bill, I sold my YSL make-up bag of Clinique to a British girl from our bus for $150. That'll take care of dinner, I think."

"Ha, you and Yves can buy dinners for the next three days with that."

Jim studied his daughter and then said, "When we get to Sri Lanka, if you're interested, I'll take you to an orphanage where you may want to volunteer for the time we're there."

Kristen searched her father's face, looking for the usual parental loophole. "Dad, are you serious? That would be so totally awesome."

An hour later, after 15 orders of *naan* and chicken *tikka* had been consumed free of the constraints of etiquette and decorum, Kristen hugged the last little girl goodbye at the door and stood waving until they were all out of sight.

"Miss Rivers?" It was the tired waiter pointing to a heap of clothing. "These you are forgetting?" Amid the scattered food bits and ice cream goo on every surface, Kristen's Ray-Bans, a Lululemon top, and her favorite Jimmy Choo's were piled onto a chair.

She stared at the designer items for several moments before turning and running upstairs to bed.

"You will not stop them from dying. At best, you will stop them from dying today."

Aude Mermilliod, **Le Chœur des femmes**

The Good Doctor

It's a humid, hot afternoon in Northern India and Krishan is anxious to get his elderly parents into their rental car for the five-hour journey back to Delhi.

A cousin's wedding in Chandigarh has consumed three days and nights, giving his uncle, the bride's father, ample time to impress the 400 guests with his largesse. As usual, everyone is on Indian time, taking twice as long to do the simplest tasks. Chaos reigns even with servants and gofers, so by three o'clock, Krishan's patience is wearing thin.

He's a surgeon living and practicing in California for 20 years and has come home to bring his parents to the wedding. His father is nearly blind, and his mother suffers from various ailments. They could not

IN ANY GIVEN ROOM

have traveled on their own. As the eldest son, this is his time-honored duty, and he would not have dreamed of refusing them. He takes his father by the arm.

"*Pitaji*, please, we must get moving. I don't want to drive at night on these roads."

"Yes, yes, *beta*, we are just coming, don't worry."

His parents embrace the relatives for the third time and, loaded with departing boxes of sweets, finally climb into the Indian Ambassador sedan. There are no seat belts or headrests and little insulation from the relentless heat, but the car has air conditioning that will work for the first two hours at least.

Maya, his favorite aunt, comes around to the driver's door and gives him a warm kiss on the cheek. "Thank you, *beta*; you are a good son for bringing them. God bless you."

He smiles with genuine affection. Aunty Maya had been the lone positive voice years ago when he wanted to study medicine in the US. Without her unwavering support, he might never have achieved his dream.

From the age of seven, the family legend goes, Krishan had known his destiny. "I want to save people's lives, Pitaji," he announced one morning at breakfast.

"How will you do that, beta?" his amused father had asked.

"I'm going to school to become a 'sturgeon,'" he declared, standing to give the announcement the maximum importance it deserved.

Until his large, extended family saw him off at the Delhi airport on his twentieth birthday, he had grown up being called the future family 'sturgeon' at every opportunity.

Krishan had saved many lives in his twenty working years. Seeing how quickly fate can turn, he had grown cautious with his two sons the day he lost a child on the operating table for the first time. Distracted in play, the girl rode her tricycle into traffic.

After telling the parents and grandparents huddled in the waiting room the worst news imaginable, he had driven to Mt. Tamalpais and sat on the summit until dawn, railing at God. He questioned if he could handle the pain of losing anyone else, much less another child.

Growing up in India, where children are not named until one year old because so many die before that milestone, Krishan had a broad and profound view of how precious all life was.

On his visit to India, five years before, he'd helped a doctor friend outside of Delhi who visited villages to remove cataracts from patients. It was a simple operation but changed a person completely. Seeing the joy on older people's faces when they could finally see their grandchildren was worth everything.

It was a sad irony that he could do nothing for his own father's blindness. Glaucoma had no cure; his father's doctor had not caught it in time.

But on this hot afternoon, his only thought is to get his parents home to New Delhi before nightfall. Highway 1, India's primary artery, is one of the most dangerous highways in the world. His uncle tells him of a parallel back road that is much safer, and he can pick up Highway 1 again, just 20 miles outside Delhi. With a required tea break and several bathroom stops, the trip could easily stretch to five or six hours, so haste is essential.

Waving goodbye, Krishan pulls out onto one of the many broad avenues of Chandigarh. Unique in all of India, Chandigarh is a relatively new city designed by the French architect and urban planner Le Corbusier to replace the city of Lahore, which was lost to Pakistan after the partition in 1947.

If only more of India's cities could be this safe and pleasant, Krishan muses as he reluctantly leaves the orderly traffic and turns onto the hectic main highway. He'll have to stay on this for several miles before turning onto the country road his uncle recommended.

After being passed by motorcycles and cars on both sides, with drivers oblivious to traffic rules, he shakes his head in dismay as they honk in irritation at his steady 65 miles per hour.

Krishan's parents quickly fall asleep as he checks his map and finds the turn-off without a problem. The rural road is well paved and shaded with eucalyptus trees for several miles. To his relief, local bicycle and tractor traffic soon disappear, and he finds himself alone, free to speed up. Several hours later, after tea and another restroom break, Krishan is pleased to find they are ahead of schedule. He helps his parents re-settle in the backseat and pulls out, heading south to Delhi. His father chats for a few minutes and then drops off to sleep.

As he passes small villages, his thoughts move ahead to his departure in a few days. He has a busy work schedule in the coming weeks, and his oldest boy, Ashok, will soon be packing for college in the fall. His son has shown an interest in medicine, and he smiled at the possibilities.

Krishan finds he rarely has a day to spare, but he's glad he's made time for this trip. His parents are getting on, and every visit is precious.

A hovering layer of wood smoke a mile ahead signals another small village surrounded by wheat and millet fields. A lone figure is walking towards the cluster of houses on the road's right shoulder. As Krishan gets closer, he can see a very elderly man bent almost to his waist, walking with the aid of a long wooden staff. He's dressed in the standard village garb; loosely wrapped turban, dhoti, and long cotton tunic. As Krishan slows to pass, he sees two young men leaning against one of the houses, watching his car.

He taps his horn and swings to the left, giving the villager as wide a berth the road allows, but, inexplicably, the older man, who has walked in a straight line for almost half a mile, suddenly veers hard to the left.

There is no place to go. Irrigation ditches border the road on both sides. Braking in the last second is futile. At 40 miles an hour, the man is hit straight on, and his frail body is thrown 30 feet in front of the car.

Horrified, Krishan skids to a stop and leaps out, shouting to his parents to stay in the car. He runs to the villager, but even as he does, he knows it's a severe injury. There's a faint pulse, but the damage to the man's skull leaves little doubt that he needs immediate transport to a hospital. On the road, empty, tattered sandals are frozen in silent stride.

Krishan's mother begins getting out of the car just as they see a crowd of villagers with long wooden poles shouting and running toward the car.

He's been gone from India for 25 years, but he knows what's happening. Village justice is primitive and final; if the mob reaches them, they will be beaten to death.

For one long agonizing moment, Krishan looks from his mother's face to the man lying on the road to the approaching men shouting, "Murderer, murderer!"

"Get in the car!" he orders as he slides behind the wheel. As he guns the engine and shoots forward, several poles land on the trunk and roof of the car, but they get away unscathed.

Shocked speechless, they ride in tense silence, looking back for motorcycles in pursuit. Krishan slowly shakes his head, over and over.

"Beta," his anguished mother finally murmurs, laying a hand on her son's rigid shoulder, "there was nothing you could have done. We saw it with our own eyes. It was an accident; he walked in front of you at the last possible second."

As they approached the outskirts of New Delhi, his mother thought she heard weeping. But perhaps it was just the wind.

"Be as intellectual as you like about it, but India is brilliantly mad. And if you want to love it, you have to hate it first."

Simon Dring

The Guru With Blue Eyes

I'd been in India for nine hours. Not in the countryside viewing exotic flora and fauna or in a Bangalore museum studying 1,200-year-old statues entwined in erotic embrace. No, I was in my hotel bed, deep in the sleep of jet lag, like a total slug.

Leaving my parents, brother, and the rest of the clan waving forlornly while I marched to the plane at the San Francisco Airport had been easy—at 22, I couldn't wait to escape. My dad was disappointed, and my mom was confused, but they wore their public faces for the relatives, with no one but me the wiser. My older brother, Rick, summed it up the night before over our last beer.

"Hey, bro, not everyone needs a degree. Go to

India, find yourself; if this guru cat can clear the fog that passes for your brain, then I guess it's worth it." Rick cut to the chase with ease.

Dad and I were always at loggerheads. He wanted my life planned and structured like his. College, then four honorable years in the navy, followed by a job, then marriage, then a house, then kids, then a scheduled retirement in August of '69. Perfect for him, a prison for me. Two nights before, he made his final attempt to talk me out of my trip.

"Son, this is going to kill your mother. Kids have come back from those Asian countries addicted to LSD and pot and robbed of everything they own. Rick and you are all we have. Please don't do this."

I told him that if I looked up boring in the dictionary, there he'd be. He turned away, but I hadn't cared. I was suffocating in his tract house, in his tract town, and in his tract life. The world was calling.

My summer jobs and Christmas gifts would cover the basics, and selling my motorcycle took care of the ticket. Not one penny from my parents. I swaggered with self-righteousness. The final act of defiance was refusing to cut my long brown hair. Hey, if it was good enough for John Lennon.

Only Rick knew I was making a beeline for an ashram. Ever since hearing Guru Bhagwan Ji speak at a Santa Cruz Self Awareness Festival the year before, I'd dreamed of becoming his disciple. Both his books called to me. They also called to hundreds of other

Americans who were already at his ashram, and I felt like the ship was pulling away.

I had the saffron robe and rope sandals that all new disciples wore. Chapter one~ *"We must separate ourselves from the shallow trappings of the material life."*

Every night I burned candles and tried to meditate according to the rules in chapter four of the guru's first book. But the Bhagwan was right; my western mind was jumbled and disorganized, my thoughts scattered. I had so much to learn and felt sure it would fall into place once I was in his presence, under his guidance, breathing the same air, eating the same food, walking the walk—a universe away from anal San Jose and my white-bread family.

The phone pulled me out of bottomless sleep. Groping in the dark, I finally stopped the shrill double ring. "Hello?"

An Indian, speaking heavily accented English, greeted me. "Mr. Keeneth Hanseen, isn't it?"

"Yeah, who's this?"

"Ahhh, the eternal question."

"Well, it's one of my eternals. Are you from the ashram?"

"I am from many things, but tonight, in this life, I will be from the ashram."

"Great! I'll be right down. Give me five to change, okay?"

"Give you five? Sir, at the ashram, we're not using currency or other methods of bribery."

The advice from the Indian Consulate in San Francisco kicked in—do not use slang; always speak in simple, complete sentences.

"Five minutes, I'll be down in five minutes, and the name is Ken."

"Mr. Keen, time has little relevance; five or fifty minutes, no matter. I'm just waiting."

I dug out my saffron robe, but the cotton looked like a ball of crushed aluminum foil—my jeans would do for now. After one last glance at the soft bed, TV, and thick carpet, I eagerly turned out the light and closed the door on my previous life.

If I didn't count the stifling heat at midnight or the funny three-wheeled taxi with one board left as flooring, my first surprise was the attractive blond accompanying my greeter, Pavan. She neither offered her name nor made eye contact, relaying all her comments through the Indian guy. She seemed to oversee Pavan and would occasionally correct him when he tried explaining my upcoming orientation.

Our little three-wheeler teetered through heavy traffic with blaring horns and enough pollution to kill off any asthmatic. The driver ignored red lights, and wandering cattle had the right of way. A troop of screeching monkeys rushed our taxi, but Pavan and Blondie swatted them with sticks the driver supplied, and they scattered. *Rick would love this*, pinged through my thoughts before a truck squeezed us into near paste against a battered bus.

"Is it always like this at midnight?" I asked Blondie.

Pavan answered, "The outer world is chaos; you will soon be at the ashram, and peace will enfold you."

"Great, can't wait!" They ignored me for the rest of the ride.

At the 2 a.m. orientation, the other newbies and I learned that women and men kept separate quarters and mixed only during meals. Book one outlined the guru's philosophy. *Mixing the sexes upsets our seven chakras and interferes with our quest for enlightenment~* Chapter One. Carnal thinking rocked the boat.

By the time I'd had my head shaved with a rusty straight-edge razor, those shots back home were making sense. I plunked down the final payment for the first three months, had the latrines pointed out, and was shown my upper bunk in a primitive shack for eight guys. It was 4 a.m., and my boat was in dry dock.

One hour later, a loud gong a foot from my head announced morning meditation. My seven roommates, Yanks but for a Swede and two Japanese brothers, helped me get my robe tied and draped. Then we were off to the "Garden of Tranquility." *Meditation brings us to our center and releases impurities of thought and mind~* Chapter Two.

The sky was still black, and the air warm and damp. Our group had one candle to light the path, while ahead and behind, other groups walked single file, with only the rustle of robes and shuffling of sandals to announce our presence. At last, I would see and maybe hear our guru.

According to the Swede, there was a small army of junior gurus (JGs) who ran the day-to-day of the ashram. One JG stood to announce that Guru Bhagwan Ji was bringing light to Europe and would return in three weeks.

For a second, the question of where he stayed when he traveled tugged at me while having my first shower in an outdoor stall loosely sided with bamboo poles. The bucket overhead had several holes punched through the bottom. Another disciple stood on a bamboo ladder and poured the two allowed portions of water into the holey bucket, which gave me about 60 seconds to rinse off the soap.

Only after meditation, bed making, and floor-sweeping, followed by a shower and 30 minutes of reading the guru's teachings, were we allowed to walk silently to the Pavilion of Sustenance, where breakfast waited.

To free ourselves from trivial cravings, food must be simple~ Chapter Two. That first meal was something else. I'd never in my life had cauliflower and eggplant for breakfast. And whoever heard of yogurt first thing in the morning? But there it was on the food line—a big scoop each of spicy vegetables, white rice, and yogurt, what the locals called curd. Pitchers of hot tea sat on the tables.

I was so hungry, anything would have tasted good, and I'd almost, but not entirely, forgotten that the ladies would join us. All their tables were on the far side of the open-air pavilion. Every girl had a long braid down her back, and only a few looked our way. One cute little redhead caught my eye, and we smiled. Then, she waved her spoon at me before the Indian girl next to her looked up and gave me the evil eye.

And so, my quest for enlightenment began. Daily, with the sun coming up over the papaya and guava trees that ringed the ashram, we had two hours of mandatory weeding in the vegetable gardens and another hour of latrine duty before our first break for cold water or a cup of tea.

I was perpetually exhausted and lost ten pounds in the first month. When would we listen to our guru, any guru, lecture, and enlighten? Sure, we all had to pitch in, but if I wanted to work this hard, I could've stayed home and gotten a job that paid me decent money. I'd spent every cent to my name to come here. As Mom hugged me goodbye, she tucked a twenty into my jean pocket, and that was it.

Two months in, I approached Blondie and asked when we would hear our guru. She looked around and whispered that we had to complete ten weeks of initiation before we could be in his presence. She squeezed my arm and added, "Since you've been doing so well, I will allow you to work in the guru's office and be closer to his essence."

Another thought wormed its way across my righteous path; did my 65-wpm typing skills listed on my application have something to do with it? But I dismissed the negative thinking and thanked her for the special favor.

Over 400 people were paying to be near Bhagwan Ji; some had been near him for three years. These senior disciples wore purple robes with polished wooden beads around their necks and kept to themselves. Quite a few were stunning women who wore makeup and worked in the main building.

I chalked the scene up to a well-run ashram that did good, albeit slow, work for the thousands of kids whose dreams had died with Kennedy in '63 and then were gut-punched by Viet Nam. The guru's phenomenal book sales worldwide spoke to the search for comfort and stability.

After dinner, I had to type the last of a book sales report the night before we heard Bhagwan Ji. In the office near my desk was a bathroom with a western toilet and sink; I'd used nothing this modern for months. No one was around, and I could return to work and save a long walk to the latrine. Inside the bathroom, a connecting door on the opposite wall was slightly ajar.

Wafting through the opening was the unmistakable aroma of pot, and then I heard low laughter. None of this was my business. Didn't chapter eight outline being responsible only for our conduct, destiny, and path?

But I'd been working my butt off for the past three sweltering months, weeding, digging, sweeping, typing, and eating the same meatless food at every meal to clear my body of trivial cravings—outlined in chapter two.

Someone was having a party not outlined anywhere. What gave?

Was it my western upbringing that encouraged imagination and curiosity, or the nagging feeling I'd come all this way for nothing? Mixed in that bag was the reason I turned off the light and pushed open the door.

On a platform covered in tie-dyed spreads, my esteemed guru, fifty pounds heavier than his book cover photo, and three of the prettiest JG's, sprawled in mindless abandon. The senior disciples wore purple bikinis with "kiss this chakra" in silver printed on the bottoms. Busy with their trivial cravings in the thick pot smoke, dim candlelight, and sitar music, I went unnoticed.

The man I thought of as my spiritual savior was chuckling, "The amazing stupidity of these foreign idiots is making me rich."

Two girls rubbed oil on his back; one asked when they were going to his Château in Provence.

"Don't worry, don't worry, all in good time," he smiled as he patted her head like an obedient lap dog.

Backing away, I closed the connecting door and sat at my desk to think. One of Dad's sayings came to me and settled my thoughts; *for every rat you see, there are ten you don't.*

Taking the shortest route to my shack, I grabbed my camera, Rick's farewell gift, and hurried back to the office. It was after 10 p.m., and only the gate guards were still awake; I would photograph the guru and run. My return ticket, passport, and Mom's twenty were safe in a travel pouch I kept on me.

Easing the connecting door open, I found the group stoned into oblivion. Walking around the platform, I shot a dozen photos, keeping the guru's face front and center in every frame.

For Blondie, a note about an emergency at home would head off any alarm over my empty bunk. A quick search of the office files revealed deeds to the chateau, a London flat, and a beach compound on the Costa del Sol in Spain. With registration slips to three Mercedes and two Silver Shadow Rolls Royces, and bank records of accounts holding over seven million dollars, my camera recorded the bitter icing on this sour, rotten cake.

Instead of elation, a wave of self-revulsion rolled over me. What a fool, a laughingstock, a complete and total idiot. On that one point, the jackass stoned out of his twisted mind was right.

My plane landed at SFO at the civil hour of 1 p.m. on a Saturday in October. I'd called Rick collect during a New York stop but expected no one to meet me. For the twenty-six-hour flight, I'd struggled with what to say to the three people who loved me, who supported my dreams, no matter how wacko or out in left field. The three people I had treated with contempt and smug superiority, the three people who gave a damn.

During the four-hour layover in New York, I sent the film and this story to the New York Times features editor, whose writers had covered several pieces on the phony guru. Let them do what they would. It was all I knew to partially right the wrong done to my bunkmates, the cute little redhead, Blondie, and all the others who had put their lives on hold, who had invested their all and so wanted to believe.

Then, I opened the lobby doors, and there they were. Dad had lost weight. Mom began crying and hugging me, running her hands over my face and shaved head, not quite believing I was still alive. Rick pounded me on the back, mumbling things only Rick could mumble. My dad was still and quiet, an island of calm in the maelstrom of shouts and boisterous laughter as families reunited.

For three months, I'd lived in Oz, where nothing was as it seemed. Looking at him now, for the first time in years without filters, I saw my father's genuineness, core decency, and compassion I had never allowed myself to acknowledge or admit. In my arrogance, I had turned my back and looked a world away for these very things.

"Dad..." was all I could choke out. I threw my arms around him, and we hugged for a long time. Then, he gently pulled back, and holding my shoulders, he looked at me with his clear blue eyes and said the only words that mattered, "I've missed you, son, welcome home."

"Be not so bigoted to any custom as to worship it at the expense of truth."

Zimmerman

The Brahmin and The Dalit

A compact man of 5 feet 8 inches in height, Vijay Sharma had a medium-fair complexion and a serene expression that projected confidence to those who had the occasion of his services. Only Brahmins conducted weddings, funerals, dedications of buildings, and blessings for new babies.

This afternoon, he placed the Brahmin red powder mark on his forehead with extra care, for he was going to the bank. A most fortuitous event had occurred, and now money was, at last, in his pocket. It was his karma taking charge, though everyone who knew him would assume that this was his due because of his high birth.

Like most Brahmins, Sharma had been raised to believe that he was superior in every way. He was from the priestly caste of pundits, the ones closest to the gods. Only a Brahmin brought good fortune to an event by being there. Hinduism and tradition also charged Brahmins with the duty of keeping themselves pure.

The most orthodox among them would not allow the shadow of a Dalit to fall across their persons. In his grandfather's time, servants walked ahead, announcing that a Brahmin was coming, and the less worthy always made way.

Untouchables were also called Dalits, which meant suppressed in the ancient Sanskrit language. Once, as a youth, he had brushed up against a low caste man on a busy street. His grandfather demanded two days of purification ceremonies to rid him of the taint. It was years before the shame faded, and his family forgave him.

Sharma believed it was his right to make others wait. If the appointment was for three p.m., no one expected him to arrive at three sharp or even at half-past three. He was, after all, a Brahmin, and another person's inconvenience was never his concern. As customers saw him, heads bowed slightly, and eyes lowered in respect as he approached the bank's counter.

He initially dismissed the disturbing news that some members of the Dalit caste now held respectable jobs that should rightfully go to upper castes. Then, he recalled that one of those people lived close to him in his neighborhood -- his world was tilting out of balance.

As Mr. Sharma left his house earlier, he observed the man walking to work. No sense of shame, the man was brazen, with his head held high, dressed in a tan suit and red tie as though he had a right to look like his betters. In his grandfather's time, the Dalit would have been beaten senseless.

For Sharma, the modern world of cell phones and computers affected him not, for he was a proud standard bearer for all things traditional and timeless. But when he examined his heart in the dark of night, he knew his insular world was cracking. Money was running out, and the cold hand of despair lay on his shoulder.

His son, Nishant, 17, had done exceptionally well on his board exams and was ready to register for college. The boy was his pride and joy, an extension and reflection of him, his father, and his father's father before him, for these things mattered deeply in India.

There was a way of doing things, and for Brahmins, the manner in which every part of life was played out was marked in the golden book in heaven. Mr. Sharma had never, in all his years, varied in how he conducted himself.

A recent streak of bad luck, including a wealthy relative's false promise of money, a temple assignment that fell through, and his wife's sudden illness, had left him with barely enough funds in the box under his bed to feed his family another week. His wife and son, as tradition prescribed, were unaware of this crisis. But fees for Nishant's college loomed, and his wife needed more medicine.

Suddenly, then, there was a knock on his door.

Ashok Mirza, a fellow Brahmin friend from the neighboring town, stood in his doorway with a foreigner. Sharma was suspicious of foreigners as they could not be categorized by caste. He suspected this big white man with red hair was beneath him, but his good manners prevailed, and he invited them in.

Etiquette demanded that he offer tea and snacks since Mirza was also Brahmin. But Sharma resented wasting any of his remaining supplies on this new person who kept smiling at him like a fool. Why did white people always smile and project so much energy—as though they would burst out the door and run down the road any second?

"Sharmaji," Mirza began in English, with his hands held in the submissive palms-together position, "may I present Mr. Collin Winkley from England? He's a journalist I met on the train, we got to talking, and he would like to interview you for an article he's writing for the BBC."

Sharma looked at them placidly while his mind raced. What did this mean, an article? "Mirzaji, please, what is this about?"

Winkley piped up. "A pleasure, I'm sure, Mr. Sharma. You've come highly recommended for a piece I'm writing on the changing India. How everyone is making scads of money, living well, buying cars, computers, all that."

Living well, buying cars? Mirza has no idea.

"How does this concern me exactly, Mirzaji?" Sharma found it impossible to address his remarks to this red-haired leviathan who wouldn't stop smiling and was now rummaging around in a large leather bag.

Leather? The skin of our Holy Cow in my home! Oh, Ram, we are defiled.

Mirza followed Sharma's horror-filled eyes and saw the offense of offenses, short of pulling a rump roast out of his bag and plopping it down on the table.

"Ah, um, Mr. Winkley, sir, may we continue this discussion in town at the park? I just remembered a funeral we're to conduct. Please accept my profound apologies, but we must take leave. Shall we meet tomorrow at 11 a.m.?"

Popping up out of his chair, Winkley checked his beeping phone.

"Right-o, fine with me. See you at the park's tea court at 11 a.m. sharp." He swung his big bag onto his shoulder, and before Sharma knew what was happening, the skin that touched cowhide grabbed his Brahmin hand for hearty shakes before bolting out the door. Sharma held the defiled hand and arm out from his side and sank to the floor in shock.

"Sharmaji, please let me join you in purification and prayer. Then I will tell you the wonderful news." Mirza was sincerely apologetic but couldn't contain his excitement.

"Mr. Winkley will pay you 400 pounds, not rupees, but pounds sterling for your interview!"

Sharma reeled at the amount. This sum was more than he earned in two months. The money would put Nishant in school, cover his wife's medicine, and provide a new bicycle he sorely needed. But the cost to his Brahmin soul was incalculable. He should never allow this foreign man to come near him again, who had so defiled his home.

However, he reasoned, Winkley was not an Indian. The lines were murky, but he hoped to find a loophole. After his friend left, Sharma scrubbed down the sitting room and said lengthy prayers of contrition. Finally, he consulted his holy books. Hours later, he turned the last page with a faint smile.

All he needed to do after receiving the remuneration was to put the money through its own purification ceremony, thus elevating it to a holy state. Every bill must be washed and anointed with holy oil. Then special prayers recited in his sacrosanct prayer room upstairs. Only then could he wrap the money in a clean silk cloth and take it to the bank.

Sharma kept Winkley waiting for an hour in the park. The big man was cheerfully cutting up mangos and had the colossal cheek to offer him a piece before getting down to business. Sharma answered questions, made many declarative statements on the glories of the caste system, and voiced his considerable opinions on the distribution of India's wealth while sitting on the opposite side of the picnic table to ensure his arms rested nowhere near

Winkley. At last, the agony ended, and he received a white envelope thick with money.

Two hours later and at the bank, at last, Sharma told the woman teller he needed to make a deposit. "A sizable amount," he advised with an air of importance.

"Yes, Punditji," she replied in the required respectful manner. "I'll call the manager of deposits to take your money." Only a manager or above was ranked high enough for a Brahmin.

Sharma squared his shoulders and looked around. He recognized a couple he had married the previous year and a widower whose wife's funeral he conducted last spring. They bowed in respect. His world was finally coming back into balance, and then he heard, "Sir, I'm Mr. Thacker, Manager of Deposits. May I be of assistance?"

Sharma recognized the tan suit and red tie from his neighborhood, a thought flashed to his grandfather, and his world imploded with a big hand reaching for his holy money.

"In Haryana, a state where the ratio of women to men is dismal, female foeticide is still surreptitiously advertised by slogans which announce: 'Spend rupees 1,000 today: Save rupees 100,000 tomorrow!'"

Pavan K. Varma, **Being Indian**

Saving Rita

Rita woke to morning rustlings and a low hum of voices. She kept her eyes closed a moment longer, feeling the ceiling fans' efforts to move the humid monsoon air. Sleeping through another night in a room with twenty women always surprised her. She opened her left eye just enough to read the clock above the far door. It was Rita's one marker of time unless she counted the shadows on the opaque windows. But, with nowhere to be, looking at the clock was only habit.

I've been here for 44 days, and 1000 nights, she would say when anyone new asked. Today was important; she'd been told. A new doctor was going to assess her readiness to go home. Home—what did that mean anymore?

"Rita," her mother wailed months before, "please, just meet the boy one more time; he comes from such a good family. You are sending me to my death bed, you ungrateful girl!"

Then her mother had thrown herself onto her bed, thrashing and moaning, while stealing peeks to see if Rita was buying it. The act had worked with her two older daughters but not with this one. "Sharp as a tack," Rita's father had warned his wife.

The "good boy" had been wearing a mustard plaid suit and had a pronounced underbite with oil in his hair. His mother had sucked her teeth and stared while burping and slurping her tea. It was all so hideous as to be funny had her parents not taken the proceedings seriously.

That had been just the beginning of marriage season. Six "good families" later, with six acrimonious rejections and six visits from her aunts, uncles, grandparents, and sisters to loudly complain about how she was shaming the family, Rita had developed what everyone decided to call a nervous disorder.

Reeking of rose water and Old Spice, good family number seven was seated in the parlor after depositing their shoes by the door. Rita made her modest head down and eyes averted appearance. Carrying a sandalwood tray laden with tea cakes, "She's an excellent cook," her mother recited on cue; she set the tray down and stole a look at #7. He wasn't all that bad, but then, while bent over with the tray, she looked at his feet for some reason. His crumpled socks had large holes where his inch-long toenails had cut through, and Rita began to laugh.

Both parents smiled, hoping to be let in on the joke. But the boy had noticed her glance downward and knew. He blushed beet red and tucked his feet back under the couch. This triggered more laughing, and Rita, knowing all was lost, pointed to the source of the amusement as she held her stomach and bent double. Her parents were aghast. #7 and his parents were so horrified that they harrumphed with all their remaining dignity and stormed out as far as the front door, where they had to stop and put on their shoes.

The family priest was called after Rita locked herself in her room and refused to speak or eat for two days. Not wanting to break tradition, Rita's mother served the priest numerous cups of tea and a hearty lunch but sent him away when his prayers and advice did nothing. Finally, her favorite cousin, Anil, who privately agreed with her on the ills of arranged marriages, was asked to reason with her.

Alarmed over her behavior and the curious questions from neighbors, who diligently monitored the priest's and relatives' comings and goings, her parents agreed with Anil to stop talk of marriage for the time being.

"Just come out and be normal," her mother pleaded.

But what Rita didn't know was her parents had already arranged to admit her to the Happy Hills Clinic for Women. Only her father or a husband could sign her release. What the family didn't know and would be shocked to learn; upon arrival at Happy Hills, she had never been happier—but happiness is always relative.

Mrs. Singh, two cots down, had begun her tea-making for the morning. Her sister had brought her a small portable stove and tea kettle. Nalini Roy, three cots down and across, contributed the tea leaves and sugar, and Rita always supplied the rusks, dry, sweet toasts everyone had with their first cup of the day. The three ladies would sit huddled together on Mrs. Singh's sturdy rope cot and discuss the latest clinic gossip.

"Have you seen the new doctor?" Nalini asked with trepidation. Beaten by her spouse and mother-in-law for years, she had finally taken a broom handle one night to her drunken husband. Numerous old bruises on her back and legs had saved her from going to prison. So here she was until he wanted her back. She, too, was very content.

"Don't worry, Nalini, just act goofy, and whoever the doctor is, he'll keep you another year," Mrs. Singh advised, with a sideways head wobble. "God willing, God willing," Nalini murmured.

Usha Kaur, four cots up, had been in their group until they caught her stealing tea from Nalini's locker and selling it to one of the women on Ward C. The Crying Ward was the unofficial name the staff used, but it was the Comfort Ward among the patients, who spent hours sitting quietly together with arms entwined.

C Ward held the women who had lost their hold on reality after being bullied into having another abortion, giving up a newborn daughter to an orphanage, or worse, watching it being carried out into a field, never to be seen again. One woman, Geeta, had been forced to watch her brother-in-law drop her newborn daughter down an abandoned well. The family said this was Geeta's punishment because everyone knew having girls was the mother's fault. Three years had passed, but Geeta still could not drink cold well water. The cot ladies didn't object to the tea going to Ward C; they minded that Usha had stolen instead of asked and, worse, had taken money for it.

The new doctor would come after breakfast that the patients made for themselves in the communal kitchen. The cot ladies always sat with several other patients from their ward. There was a rumor that elderly Mrs. Khanna, a widow, would go home soon now that her oldest son had died, and the estate had passed to her grandson, Arjun. Educated in London with modern ideas, Arjun wanted his grandma home and would spend whatever it took to keep her comfortable in her old age.

Mrs. Khanna was scared. Indian culture often viewed widows as the scourge of the family. What if they took her to Vrindavan, the holy city where thousands of widows were abandoned every year, to become servants of idle priests? She hadn't seen Arjun in several years and only knew he had married an

Indian woman from London. What if his wife abused her? The world was a frightful place for Mrs. Khanna.

Rita realized these women had done nothing to deserve their sad situations. She was lucky and had made an important decision over the past week. An arranged marriage was not in her future, and she had been profoundly affected by this experience.

After her shower, while sewing a button onto her nightgown, the head nurse came in with a clipboard. It was time for her assessment. Rita took her hall pass to room 4A and knocked on the heavy wooden door. "Enter," a male voice ordered. She opened the door and found a young man seated behind a battered desk. He looked up from a file and smiled pleasantly. *He's quite attractive; why couldn't he be older? God, this is going to be so embarrassing.*

"Rita Bavra? Please sit down. I'm Doctor Kumar, and I'm here today to assess your progress." He smiled warmly and then asked, "Rita---mmm, were you named for the actress?"

"Yes, my father liked Rita Hayworth a lot, and my mother didn't object to the name, so..."

"Ah, my parents liked her movies also; they were trendy in India. I see here that you have been with the clinic for over six weeks. Tell me about your time here and what you want to happen."

Rita was prepared to dislike him but found him easy to talk to, and he had a warmth and gentleness that drew out her thoughts. She told him about her family and their old-fashioned views. Their refusal to understand her need to decide whom she married and the men they kept inviting to look her over like a prized cow.

She even told him about #7's holey socks-- and how angry and hurt she was that her father had sent her away. She confessed she liked the clinic and the friends she had made. They talked about things she could never discuss with her conservative parents.

He understood, he said, with a smile, as his family was similar. His older brother wanted a love marriage with a girl he'd met at university. There had been a huge row. It had taken months, despite his parents having traveled the world and lived in modern Singapore for years, but finally, they relented.

Rita was charmed by Dr. Kumar. She had never had a real conversation with a man outside the family before. Were all men like this? No, instinct told her he was different. Maybe it was just his training—to talk to people and get them to open up. Yes, that was probably it. Even so, she looked forward to their Tuesday and Friday meetings with butterflies in her stomach.

Eagle-eyed Mrs. Singh noticed Rita's extra care with her hair and clothes but said nothing. After discovering Mrs. Singh was exchanging love letters with her college sweetheart, the man she had wanted to marry but her parents had rejected, her in-laws engineered her being committed to the clinic for being "mentally off." Her husband and in-laws never came to visit, but the man she had always loved came every evening. Mrs. Singh finally understood joy.

"Rita, if you don't object, I thought we would sit in the garden for our session today; the weather is so pleasant." Rita's heart fluttered. Dr. Kumar led the way, and they found an empty bench under a shady tree. Forty minutes later, Rita got up to leave, but Dr. Kumar gestured to sit back down.

"Rita, we've reviewed your progress, and based on our meetings, I'm recommending that you be released to your parents later this week." Rita was stunned, but there was more.

"This is quite a week for change," he continued in a soothing tone, "as I have accepted a position with a hospital in the US and will be leaving the clinic next week." Rita could only stare at his face in shock. She thought she saw regret in his eyes, but he smiled and took her hand. "I know you will handle whatever life gives you, Rita. You're a remarkable person and stronger than you give yourself credit for." Rita was crushed. He was so perceptive; he knew her most personal thoughts. She needed him; how could he abandon his patients like this?

With gritty self-control, she looked into his eyes, "I wish you a safe journey Dr. Kumar and much success. Thank you for everything; I'll be fine."

He walked her back to her ward, talking all the while of how ready she was to leave and how she had impressed him. He shook her hand in parting, holding it an extra few seconds, and then he was gone. Somehow she got through the remaining days, and when her parents arrived, she hugged the cot ladies, Mrs. Khanna and Geeta, goodbye, barely managing to get to the car without breaking down.

The entire Bavra clan was at the house to welcome Rita home. There was a black forest cake, the current rage, and her favorite, a clear, small sign that her parents were trying to meet her partway. Cousin Anil finally got her alone on the porch and told her she looked terrific. Was she ready to get back to everyday life? She pondered the question so long that Anil got nervous and changed the subject.

A week later, her father announced that friends from his university days in Bombay were coming for dinner. Rita hardly heard or cared but went through the ritual of dressing in her best sari of peacock blue silk and even put fragrant chameli (miniature tube roses) in her hair to please her anxious mother. She heard car doors slamming near the front gate but let her parents do the greeting and seating. Reluctant to go in and have to put on a cheerful face, Rita slipped out the side door and sat on the porch swing for a few minutes, breathing in the roses and honeysuckle.

"Rita dear," her father called her affectionately to come meet his friends. She couldn't delay another minute without being rude. With a resigned sigh, she walked down the hall and entered the living room. A friendly-looking older couple sat on the couch with an expectant air about them. A pretty girl about 18 sat next to the mother, and standing near the open window was Dr. Kumar.

"This is our youngest daughter, Rita. She's been away but fortunately has returned just in time to meet our oldest friends," her father beamed. "Rita, meet Mr. and Mrs. Kumar, daughter Sheela, and their son, Vijay, who's leaving for America as soon as his parents find him a wife, ha ha!"

With all eyes riveted on him, Vijay stepped forward and took her hand, "How do you do?" There was a mischievous twinkle in his eye as Rita dutifully dropped her head, effectively hiding the electric thrill that shot through her. Then her eyes rested on a pair of very new, smart socks with a small gold #8 stamped over each big toe.

"You can't cross the sea merely by standing and staring at the water."

Rabindranath Tagore

Anjali's Wedding

"Mummyji, how old is he? I don't want an old man for a husband."

"He's rich; that's all you need to know. Give him sons, and your work will be done. You'll have servants, a car, and a big house. More than I had at 16."

"I'm scared, Mummy. I don't know how to be a wife." Anjali began whimpering.

"Stop it; you're ruining your makeup. Have you any idea what the Delhi beautician cost us? His family wants a pretty girl with a fair complexion, so don't smear the makeup; we paid to make you at least three shades lighter."

Anjali stood still while her mother and aunt lifted the heavy wedding *garara* skirt over her head and tied the waist corset snugly across her stomach. She held her arms out obediently while her mother placed a dozen red wedding bangles on each wrist and inserted the heavy gold nose ring that only brides wear.

"Auntyji, have you seen him? Is he handsome?" she asked when they finished. Her mother and aunt exchanged glances.

"Looks aren't everything. What matters is a good family, and you're a smart girl, so don't worry." Her aunt gave her a perfunctory pat on the head.

The two women helped her finish dressing in a short red top, a tissue silk veil with a gold border, purple and red silk slippers, and her grandmother's heavy 22K gold necklace with diamonds and rubies. Her mother placed matching antique Jhumka earrings in her pierced ears. Outside, Anjali could hear a hired brass band playing wedding music off-key as it marched to the groom's hotel to fetch him for the ceremony. The groom's male relatives followed along by torchlight, dancing and singing.

"Mummyji, I'm feeling sick, and it's so hot. I need water."

"Can't you cope with anything?" her mother snapped. "What about your father and me? We've slaved to find a suitable match for you. The boy's father is prominent in Toronto; he can help your brother get a proper position. Your dowry has drained us, and all you do is complain."

"Sorry, Mummy, but I'm hot. These clothes are

heavy. You said not to move; give me water, then I'll be still."

"Roshan, *pani!*" her mother shouted. The servant boy hurried in with a plastic water bottle on a tray and bowed slightly while his eyes darted to Anjali.

"Here's your water; now get up. The priest is waiting. Remember what I told you, no smiling, no looking around like a fool. When your new husband lifts your veil, look up, and then you can smile a little." Nodding obediently, Anjali quickly tucked the small bottle into her waistband.

Leaning on her aunt and mother, she entered the hot, stuffy room that reeked of incense and sandalwood. Two hundred pairs of eyes turned to watch Anjali slowly walk to the priest sitting on a raised platform. Flute music played while everyone stared at her hidden behind the veil. Two slow ceiling fans brought little relief.

Anjali sneaked a peek at the groom, but his ceremonial turban had so many strings of tiny flowers hanging over his face she couldn't see any of his features. Her aunt pushed her down gently to sit next to the stranger looking intently at his feet.

The priest recited prayer after prayer and, quoting from the *Bhagavad Gita*, warned Anjali to look upon her husband as a god. Before circling the couple's heads with his blessings, he predicted a dozen children. Anjali followed the groom seven times around the ceremonial fire burning in a coconut shell. Her mother and aunt whispered, "stand there, take the scarf, turn here," as she walked.

An hour, then two crawled by. Anjali thought she would faint from the heat and discomfort of the hard floor. Her mind wandered as the priest droned on. She looked for a friendly face in the sea of strangers. Then she saw Roshan leaning against the wall at the back, smiling hopelessly.

Suddenly her mother said, "Stand up and meet your husband, Tarik."

As he lifted her veil to reveal her face, she saw it all—the gray hair mixed with black, his missing teeth, his breath smelling of liquor, and something rotten. He smiled to impress the crowd, took her wrist, and said, "Let's go eat, and then we can leave. I've got calls to make to Canada."

Anjali couldn't ignore the whispers and smirks. "She's 16, and he's 43 years old."

In the wedding car, festooned with strings of marigolds and iris, Anjali stared out the window as he made a call to Toronto. Speaking in English for privacy, he said, "Hey bro, yes, the girl's tasty looking but village simple. I'll spend a few days breaking her in before dumping her at her hick parents, packing the loot, and catching Air Canada Flight 290. Yeah, the dowry's good, over thirty thousand Canadian. We can buy the Tesla we've wanted with the two you got last year. We'll talk soon."

Anjali undressed in the hotel bathroom while her new husband lay on the bed, reading his text messages. The summer heat and humidity penetrated the walls. As she entered the bedroom carrying a glass of water, Tarik reached for it. "Give me that. It's bloody hot in this damn country." Anjali complied and sat in a chair near the patio's open sliding door, smoothing her silk robe. He finished the water and wiped his mouth on his sleeve.

"I'm going outside to get some night air," Anjali said, stepping onto the balcony.

Tarik started to stand but stumbled back onto the bed. He looked at her perplexed and grunted a low laugh. "Hey, you didn't poison me, did you?" He stood and made it to her side on the tenth-floor balcony in time to clutch the low railing.

"Husbandji, were you not informed that I'm convent educated and fluent in Hindi, French, and English?"

Tarik Mehta scowled and turned to grab Anjali. She was younger and quicker and jumped back as he flailed wildly, lost purchase, and fell over the low barrier. Before calling for help, she rang her house. Roshan answered.

"I'll be home soon. Put the tea water on," she said, smiling modestly.

"Indian trait: the ability to single-mindedly pursue material benefit in the most adverse and impossible situations."

Pavan K Varma, **Being Indian**

Third Class Benefits

Kuwait, July 29th, 1990

The eight Indian couples having cocktails on the apartment balcony had been friends since first coming to Kuwait City. They were foreigners in a country that desperately needed skilled labor, and they weren't there to drive taxis or garbage trucks, though non-Kuwaitis did those jobs as well. The eight husbands were doctors or engineers of various disciplines. Most of the wives also had advanced degrees but could not work where they would have seniority over a local male.

Everyone was in Kuwait for one reason only--the pay. The money was beyond their highest expectations, and all had resigned themselves to the humiliating atmosphere and attitudes of the Kuwaiti government. Even the Somali street sweepers had priority over them.

Have a traffic accident with a local, and as an Indian, you were automatically wrong and could be arrested on the spot. All disputes with merchants ended with the Kuwaitis in the right. The recourse was simple; leave or mix only with fellow ex-pats.

Tonight, as the friends watched the sunset over the desert, thoughts were on the imminent invasion of Iraqi soldiers, and along with the balcony friends, Sushil and his wife, Tej, were anxious. They still had children at home—daughter, Neeta, 14, and son Amit, 11.

The other parents had sent their children to relatives in India, the UK, and the US, but Sushil and Tej had no close relatives. Neither parent had siblings, and both sets of grandparents had passed away. Boarding school was an option, but if anything happened to the parents in the crisis, the children would be wards of the state. Tej couldn't bear thinking of it, so the kids watched TV in the next room.

The Kuwaiti government had assured everyone that the home army was more than capable of defending the tiny country and its oil fields against Iraq. Still, the men on the balcony knew that was bitterly laughable. The local soldiers could barely direct traffic on busy holidays. The country had believed neighbor Saudi Arabia, with a much bigger army, would come to its defense, but that hope quickly died. The Saudis were worse, if possible, at insisting others do their work for them.

There were images on CNN of young Saudi men lounging around hotel pools while coalition soldiers drove by to observe the desert conflict.

So now the friends prayed the US or the UK would come to their eleventh-hour rescue. The sense of helplessness was overwhelming.

Several wives were packed and ready to leave, but panicked Kuwaitis had priority at the airport, and foreigners had to wait hours, or days, for a seat. One husband had rented a van to take two of the wives overland to Saudi Arabia and fly them out of Riyadh. But friends in that city warned that the desert highway was dangerous, with rumors of Iraqi soldiers robbing and killing unescorted travelers. Leaving by sea meant depending on Kuwaiti fishermen in rickety boats to get them safely past Iraqi patrols. Few in the group knew how to swim, so that option was shelved.

Two days after the balcony get-together, rifle fire echoed from various points around the city, but no one knew what was happening. The government television station continued to broadcast canned assurances that all was under control.

Late on the second day, the government ordered a blackout, and Tej hurried to the bazaar to buy bolts of dark cloth for the windows. Sushil returned from work and assured his family he was not going back until everyone was safe. He took Tej into their bedroom and showed her the gun and box of shells he had purchased.

One day later, Iraq began bombing Kuwait City.

The children were frightened. Who was coming to help? Both armies' movements were played out hour by hour on CNN and BBC. Kuwait's defenses were a global laughingstock. How could the world watch and let the country be destroyed?

But, the family at 24 Rue de Sultana had more pressing concerns. Sushil and several of the husbands were helping each family board up their windows and sandbag their balconies. The bombing, for some convoluted reason, began at around 3 p.m. and stopped before dark. Whatever the logic, everyone was grateful for the predictability. A day later, the men had finished with Sushil's flat and left to help a friend one block away.

Tej fixed the children a light lunch and had just lit candles in the blacked-out bedrooms when there was pounding at the door. Her gut said it was no one she knew, and from the peephole, she could see a patch of unfamiliar camouflage. The children held each other on the couch as a man shouted in Arabic to open the door.

Where was the gun? Sushil had taken it with him, thinking the friends might run into an Iraqi patrol. The frantic realization of how foolish they were flashed across her mind as she told the children to be brave. Then she opened the door.

Three young Iraqi soldiers with machine guns barged forward, forcing her back into her living room. Tej hurried to sit between her son and daughter and held them to her. *We could die here;* she thought as they stopped before her and barked something in Arabic.

French is a common second language in the Middle East, so she tried, saying she didn't understand what they wanted. The leader repeated the question in rough French.

"Any Kuwaiti scum here?"

Relief flooded through Tej. "No, no, we're Indian. Please, look for yourself," she implored, pointing to the hallway, praying Sushil would not return.

The soldiers hurried to the bedrooms, where the candlelight created grotesque shadows on the walls. Tej and the children trembled as the men pawed through their things. Drawers were yanked open, and breakables crashed to the floor. One man laughed at something, and then they swaggered out with a pillowcase full of the family's property.

Neeta began crying. The men rarely saw females without headscarves; they stared at her and her mother. She buried her head under her mother's shawl. The soldiers looked around the living room, gauging if they could carry anything else when someone shouted from the outer hall, and they suddenly hurried out.

Tej and the children sat rigid with fear as the soldiers kicked in doors and neighbors pleaded for mercy. Were soldiers invading their friend's home where Sushil was? When he returned by a back stairway an hour later, the family cried in relief that everyone was still alive and unhurt.

The husbands, seeing the army patrols, had hidden in a building under construction; then watched helplessly as the Iraqis shoved blindfolded Kuwaitis onto a truck. The worst that could happen had arrived.

"I can't do this, Sushil. We've got to get out of this madness; the next Iraqi could just as well shoot everyone!"

They'd been naïve to depend on others. But had they waited too late? Sushil got on the phone, relieved it was still working and called a British friend. The American and British communities in Kuwait City had their combined social club and often invited the Indian group to their gatherings.

Kurt Michaels, the highest-ranking Brit in age and experience, answered the phone. Sushil laid out their problem; how many Indians needed to get out and how much everyone could pay for the help. Kurt said their people were devising an exit plan, and he would get back to him in an hour.

Sushil called their friends and told them to pack one small shoulder bag, each with only the barest essentials, but include as much food and water as possible as they would be on the road for a while. They must be ready to bolt out the door as soon as Kurt signaled.

The bombing would start at 3 p.m., which meant the Iraqi soldiers would retreat until dark. That was the logical but most dangerous time to leave the city.

Kurt called back at 2:30.

"Have everyone downstairs at your building in 20 minutes but no sooner. My company hired a security group to get us all out. We'll pick you up in a Red Cross truck convoy with an armed escort, but you realize we have no defense against the bombs, so make sure everyone knows the risks."

Sushil thanked Kurt and quickly called two friends who relayed the message. He had done all he could; now, everyone had to decide the lesser risk for themselves.

The apartment building was quiet as the family crept down the hall at 2:45. Then they saw why. Blood-smeared doors stood open with ransacked rooms beyond in the Kuwaiti neighbors' flats.

Their friends came rushing into the small lobby by the back entrance. Tej's closest friend, Rani, was pregnant and close to hysteria. Her pediatrician husband gave her a mild sedative and told her to calm herself.

"Look how brave the children are," he gestured to Neeta and Amit. Several people grabbed Sushil and thanked him for arranging their escape.

"Thank Kurt, let him know how grateful you are." As he spoke, air raid sirens began to wail to the north, and a bomb exploded.

"The trucks are here, Dad!" Amit shouted as the group surged forward and crowded through the door. Three oversized, white enclosed trucks rolled to a stop with large red crosses painted on the sides and roof. Kurt jumped down with a tall American holding a machine gun and told everyone to get to the back of the first truck. A ramp dropped from the opened doors revealing benches, blankets, and several gallon water bottles. There were two portable chemical toilets.

Black screens at the top of the truck's walls covered air vents. They couldn't see anything. Everyone climbed in and found seating, but Rani began sobbing. "I can't go; all our things, I can't."

"There's no choice, my darling," her husband whispered, pulling her close as the convoy moved south, and bombs began to fall blocks behind them.

Their homes were abandoned, neighbors were missing, but everyone realized they were lucky to be alive and on their way out of the war. Twice during the seven-hour trip, they heard machine gun fire, but the convoy's speed never faltered, and by midnight they were safe in Saudi Arabia.

Some couples returned to India, and a few went to live near their relatives in England and the US, but none returned to Kuwait after the Gulf War save one.

After two years in India, Sushil and Tej, with their children, resettled in Kuwait. Despite the humiliation, dangers, instability, and proximity to Iraq, they couldn't resist the incredible pay.

"Oh, the innocent girl in her maiden teens knows perfectly well what everything means."

D.H. Lawrence

Lucky

Northern India

"Who's that man at the gate?" Anu was playing with her younger cousin, Poonam, under the big mango tree in their grandfather's yard. The servant had just removed their tea dishes when Anu looked over Poonam's shoulder and asked the question that would change her young cousin's life forever.

Before Poonam turned to look at the man, a cold dread touched the back of her neck. She was rooted in place as warmth fled her core like the outgoing tide.

The girls watched their grandfather meet the stranger and listen to his news. The soft murmurings carried sadness and finality. Their grandfather seemed to age before their eyes, and his head dropped as he shuffled slowly into the house. Poonam reached out blindly for her cousin's hand as the icy chill moved down her back.

Then a wail, piercing as the death scream of a hawk, left her mother's room, soared to the top of the mango tree, and plunged into Poonam's heart. Her father, the holder, and maker of her world, was dead.

Not until her mother returned from the cremation grounds with her clothes smelling of sandalwood smoke did Poonam finally accept he was truly gone. Days and nights blurred with the arrivals and departures of relatives and friends. Poonam and her mother, Sushma, now dressed in stark widow white, sat in blind grief as the visitors sipped tea, nibbled on cashews, and tsk, tsked with sympathy.

Soon, discussions arose about the expense of "the widow and her girl." The house belonged to the paternal grandfather. Without her father's income, Poonam, and her mother, a mere daughter-in-law, were a burden.

Sympathy inevitably shifted from the widow to the grandparents, and whispers turned to open hostility. Without a family of her own, Sushma brought out her gold wedding jewelry and offered it for her and Poonam's keep. Her father-in-law accepted it grudgingly, but since widows are considered bad luck, custom dictated she must have her meals in the kitchen after the servants had eaten. Poonam waited through each meal and ate with her mother.

Once the family beauty, full of gentle laughter and song, Sushma had faded into a white-haired apparition who roamed the house at night, begging the gods for relief. It finally came one spring day, at the bottom of the family well. More relatives, more tea, more tsking, but Poonam, beyond mere grief, had ceased to hear.

Now, the servants must go a mile to the village well for the family's water. Thank you, Mother, at least for that. I will never forget you.

Days before her fourteenth birthday, and hours after hearing her grandmother announce that she was promised in marriage to a 34-year-old third cousin, Poonam decided to leave.

Her small knapsack held her mother's tortoiseshell combs, her own thin, gold newborn bangle, and her father's watch. She wrapped a cooked potato with a stale chapatti, took a pinch of salt for luck, and left the front door open wide so her mother's spirit could escape with her. Before closing the gate for the last time, the family's youngest granddaughter picked all the pink roses from the garden and scattered the pedals in the well.

As the early morning sky turned faint lavender, Poonam sat on a stump by the main road. She was three miles from the people she had once called family, but she must go a lot further before feeling safe. Learning distances had come easy after being put to work alongside her uncle on his dairy deliveries, and bicycling with five-liter milk cans had hardened her legs and arms.

She would have to be careful and stay clear of the many dairy customers who could recognize her. Poonam's empty bed was already discovered, and the alarm would soon go out. She was, if nothing else, a good worker who required no salary.

An unaccompanied female would attract all kinds of trouble. Every Indian girl knew the rules. No eye contact with males, no smiling or laughing in public, no going about alone.

Distance first, and then a shelter of some kind, was urgent. Poonam watched a large tractor-trailer loaded with hay stop a block away. The driver got down and walked to a roadside tea house for breakfast.

Tucking her knapsack under her arm, she hurried to the back of the trailer in the early light. Checking the road for curious eyes, she jumped up and covered herself with the hay. Twenty minutes later, the tractor lurched forward, and Poonam watched with grim resolve as the familiar landmarks of her brief life disappeared from view.

As she pushed a mound of hay into a makeshift pillow, her hand brushed something hard. Digging through the hay, she found two school books discarded or forgotten by the driver's children. Her culture revered education and students were left alone on their way to and from school. With these books as props, she could move around with relative ease. The pinch of salt was already working.

By afternoon, Poonam reckoned they had covered enough distance, and while the driver stopped for another tea break, she slipped away with the books held tight to her chest.

She was in a strange town, but people looked the same or even a little better. There were more cars here and those wires on so many roofs. Her uncle called them antennas and said they were for a television box. From the lengthening afternoon shadows and fewer people on the streets, Poonam realized it had to be tea time, and she was suddenly ravenous. Unable to resist any longer, she pulled the stale chapatti and potato out of her pocket and sat down under a shade tree to eat.

Across the street and down a way, an unusual building caught her eye. There was a tall, narrow tower on top of a peaked roof. A lovely sound came from the tower as she chewed on the dry bread and potato. People started going into the double doors of the building as the ringing melody continued. Intrigued, Poonam got up and walked down to see what was happening.

The doors were open, and she could see people sitting in rows on a clean floor covered with colorful rugs. A group of women was singing in front of the people. The song was in another language, but the music was cheerful and pleasant. The singers were smiling and seemed happy. Poonam was pulled in, compelled by something beyond conscious thought. She listened to the singers, then to a man speaking in a strange tongue. Finally, as people got up, a smiling woman in a green sari came to her. In Hindi, the woman invited her to join them in the next room for tea.

She started to say no, but the woman was friendly, without any nosey questions. A few girls her age were in the small crowd, and she was still terribly hungry. Before she could think of what to do, a server handed her a big mug of steaming tea and a plate of sandwiches.

"Come, sit with my daughter and me, and we will eat together," urged the woman. Her daughter smiled and reached out to help carry Poonam's books.

It had been three years since Poonam had sat with anyone for a meal. Eating scraps alone in the kitchen had become her reality after her mother died.

Her fragile defenses broke from this unexpected kindness. Tears pooled and then dropped down her dusty cheeks. Confused and embarrassed, she studied her plate and sipped her tea.

"I'm Aunty Jain, and this is our daughter, Tia. Our church serves tea to the community every Tuesday and Friday. How good we met you today. What shall I call you, *beti?*"

"I'm, ah…my name is Lucky." *Where did that come from,* Poonam wondered. Well, the deed was done. Lucky, it was.

"Lucky, how unusual, but maybe it will prove providential. Names have such power, don't you think?"

Aunty Jain had seen the tears clearly and knew something horrible had happened to this lovely, dust-covered child with bits of hay in her hair and deep hurt in her eyes.

A new name and a new life began that afternoon. The Jains took her into their home and their hearts. She had not known family love like this was possible.

Tia became the sister she had always wanted, and Mrs. Jain helped heal the wounds left by her parents' deaths. Mr. Jain was a wise and kind man, always ready to listen to Poonam's ideas, and ended every talk with a hug.

A discreet inquiry through a private detective revealed that the grandparents had died, and Poonam's uncle and family had immigrated to Canada.

The Jains were Christians in the land of Hindus. They did not believe in joint families or arranged marriages, to Lucky's surprise and relief. Even more impressive, Aunty and Uncle strongly believed girls should go to college and become self-sufficient before marriage.

Lucky was eager to start school and soon showed her natural skills in math. By her last year of high school, Lucky's principal had convinced the Jains, now her legal guardians, that she was a brilliant candidate for the Queen's College Scholarship in Commerce, the first step in becoming a chartered accountant.

Eight years later, with her degree framed on the wall of her office, Lucky marveled at the altered path her life had taken. She would always be deeply grateful for Jain's help and love and try to repay them somehow. But, her mother's face came to her at times when she was least prepared. *Don't forget me, beti.*

On Lucky's orderly desk, a small glass box held a tiny gold bangle, two tortoiseshell combs, and a man's watch. *Never.*

Lucky had joined the government's task force on income tax reform and was the assistant district officer in charge of penalty assessments. Tax evasion was rampant in India. One day, her aid brought in a list of properties that had been seized and were going to auction in the neighboring district. She looked over the list and felt her mother's spirit nudging her to invest.

Several days later, she drove with Uncle Jain to look at the empty house and land she had chosen. The yard was weedy and neglected. A large mango tree was still bearing fruit, and the rose bush was thriving, full of pink blossoms. Ignoring a rare protest from Uncle, Lucky won the bid, and she signed the papers two weeks later.

Lucky's plans were rolling with a low-interest government loan and her considerable savings. The old house was razed, and keeping to her budget, a no-frills, two-story thirty-one-room home was built to her specs on the site. Each floor had a central social area with a kitchen attached.

Lucky had the abandoned well filled and bricked over, with a bronze plaque erected in the center. A gardener planted thirty-one pink rose bushes to circle the old well. As she walked to her car after a busy day overseeing the final touches, an older neighborhood woman approached her.

"*Beti*, tell me, what are all these loud goings on? Wait, don't I know you?"

The older woman came close and peered into

Lucky's face. "Are you not Sushma's girl? You look just like her."

The words brought Lucky to her knees. She had not heard her mother's name spoken in over 17 years. "Do I?" the heartbroken ten-year-old inside her asked.

"Yes, yes, exactly like her. Oh, *Ram*, beautiful your mother was, and with such a gentle spirit. I told your grandfather he was dead wrong to treat her that way, but he was from the old school—stupid man, so sad. Then you disappeared, but I understood, child, don't worry. It looks like you've done well. I guess your parents named you right after all."

"What do you mean?"

"You don't remember *beti*? Your pet name was given until your naming ceremony at one year old. Sushma and your father were so happy that you were born healthy; they called you Lucky until you were almost three."

After the car left, the old woman's curiosity got to her, and she walked over to the plaque. "In memory of Sushma, who died here at thirty-one years of age, bereft of husband, home, and love. May all who enter these grounds know only kindness and safety within. You are home, at last, Mataji." Over the building's entrance hung a smaller plaque; Sushma's House for Widows and Their Children.

"India is a place where color is doubly bright. Pinks that scald your eyes,
blues you could drown in."

Kiran Millwood Hargrave

Fabric Nirvana

I've always been drawn to fabric and loved cotton before it was a thing before it became expensive with its own stores and designated "pure." The sumptuous feel of silk, in all its variations, remains sublime.

My seamstress grandmother made a pink, raw silk dress for my high school graduation. She made most of my clothes until I went to college, so I spent a lot of time in fabric stores when fabric stores were everywhere, and most women sewed. Perhaps it was a portent for what was to come.

I met my husband, Gopal, in 1965, in California. For the next two years, I embraced his culture, his customs, and the beauty of craftsmanship that swirls through the unique fabrics of India.

We married in San Francisco in 1967, and four

years later, in April 1971, I stepped off the plane in New Delhi at 4 a.m. in a gray and pink silk sari borrowed from an Indian friend. To honor their customs, I first touched my mother and father-in-law's feet before saying "namaste" and giving them each a hug.

I soon realized I was in fabric nirvana. There was nothing back home to compare to the intricate block printing, the complicated tie dying, the two and three-tone Madras plaids from South India, the beautiful vine and flower patterns from Kashmir, or the fantastic cut work on everyday cotton and silk saris. I was amazed at the complex weaving on soft belts worn on slips under the sari, belts no one else would ever see but that I've saved for the beautiful work.

That April, five hours north of New Delhi, in Gopal's hometown of Patiala, it was 100 degrees with 95% humidity. The homes had no air conditioning, only ceiling fans, dependent upon the intermittent flow of electricity. Cotton was the coolest fabric in the summer; the thinner, the better.

I quickly learned I was at the mercy of my petite mother-in-law as to what I wore and how I looked. People came in rickshaws and scooters to see the white, foreign wife. In the early seventies, any foreign wife was not only a novelty but viewed as a useless white elephant.

"Can you cook Indian food?" was the bar by which my worth was measured.

Invitations to welcome their oldest son back home and to meet his wife went out to 75 people. My in-laws took me to a sari store because nothing I had was suitable. They wanted me in a dark color because I was light-complected, but I was miserable in the heat and wanted something pastel in color and lightweight. I discovered tussar silk, a cross between organza and silk, light and reasonably cool.

But Gopal's mother had the final say, so I wore thick coral silk with gold thread and my mother-in-law's heavy, gold necklace from her trousseau. I stood outside on the lawn for two hours in the steaming, muggy night, sipping hot tea while people politely circled me with either open curiosity or veiled suspicion.

Cotton, in dozens of variations, saved me that first summer. My favorite was unavailable because only men could wear the super thin, soft white cotton kurta top with a matching white pajama. White is the color of mourning for women, so I was steered in other directions. I soon found versions of thin cotton in vibrant colors and endless patterns that soothed the eye or poked the imagination.

I discovered craftswomen who did custom embroidery on evening shawls, saris, and long chiffon scarves. Embroidery appeared on cloth slippers, wool robes, pillows, and anything a needle could push through. There were inexpensive seamstresses and tailors on almost every corner, ready to make any garment with any fabric.

I began buying gifts to bring home. I gave one friend a long cotton tunic in chocolate and cream block print, and she loved it so much that I was ordered to find another for the next twenty years of visits. We were in India for nine months on that first visit, and I was never happier.

The few western women I saw in Delhi looked awkward and clumsy in shorts and dresses. I wore Indian clothes the entire time. It was all so familiar to me; how does one explain the unexplainable?

On a visit in the late 80s, we accompanied my in-laws to a girls' orphanage they supported with sweaters and tea during the winter.

A new joy and fulfillment entered my life.

Forty-two girls, who had been abandoned on street corners, tossed away by their fathers because they were female, left under train seats, and under bushes, lived together in a cold, dilapidated building

Tragedy surrounded them, yet they were full of joy whenever we arrived. Starved for affection, needing to be held, loved, and listened to, always waiting patiently for their turn to cuddle with us, they were eager for books, hungry to learn, and dreamed of going to a good school.

When we first met them, they wore donated clothes and passed these well-worn, faded garments down to the next size. I began buying for them at a discount clothing store, and when that chain went out of business, at Walmart and Target. Though I've never liked synthetic fabrics, I faced the fact that synthetics lasted longer and took more abuse than cotton and wool.

Bright sweaters were a group favorite, and the older girls did their best to care for everything we brought. The younger girls loved the boldly patterned mittens and warm socks. India has no central heating, and winters are brutal in Punjab. The orphanage management had a multitude of excuses for why they couldn't provide space heaters or hair dryers for the girls.

There was no hot water, so they washed their hair in ice-cold water all winter and had to dry it in 40 and 50-degree air. We were angry with the management, but they complained hair dryers took too much electricity. We brought winter hats and more gloves and urged them to wait for sunny days for hair washing.

Finally, when a girl reached eighteen, a boy would be found by the orphanage board, and she would be married off. For the first time in her memory, she had new clothes, new shoes, several new saris, and a complete trousseau for a modest home, which meant living with her in-laws in India.

There are streets lined with shops just for wedding decorations, sari stores just for the wedding sari or garara, a very fancy full skirt with top and veil. Some gararas, with heavy gold and silver work, can weigh 30 pounds.

When Gopal and I were married in San Francisco, I wore a green and silver sari, and he wore a deep pink silk, knee-length sherwani woven with gold thread.

His formal coat was already an antique, having been worn by his grandfather to the court of the Maharaja of Patiala.

Today, I have one-of-a-kind fabric and embroidery work packed away for safekeeping. Saris, shawls, purses, placemats, tablecloths, and bedspreads from designs and talent no longer found.

Cotton is not very durable, especially in humid weather, but we have one garment that has somehow survived decades of hot, humid summers. It's in pieces now—nothing fancy, just a little hand embroidery in white on white. But one can tell it's a baby's cotton summer kurta, what an infant would wear, what my husband wore, and what his loving mother managed to save for over 70 summers and then pass on to me, and soon, I will pass it on to our son.

Acknowledgments

India's people, and especially the children, helped build and inhabit these stories until they had to be told. Telling and publishing are opposite shores of a giant sea. As I contemplated the long journey across that sea, the book gods introduced me to novelist Ann Saxton Reh. Ann guided and advised with infinite patience, friendship, and good humor. The book would not exist without her. My gratitude to Rich and Leslie DeDora for their enthusiasm and sharp observations in reading the stories. Profound thanks to Karen Defoe, prize-winning poet and grammarian extraordinaire who knows every comma and semicolon by name. Katy Longshore is a gifted writer and editor who sees the bigger story and helped me tie gossamer ends and connect invisible dots. Karen Phillips designed a beautiful cover that captured the spirit of the stories.

Thanks to Vinod Chopra, M.D., for advice and guidance on medical and cultural matters. To Kavita Pabbi, for her infinite knowledge of arranged marriages and the inner workings of joint families. A special thank you to Pooja Bedi; from the moment we met on Diwali over 20 years ago, she became a friend who understood why the orphan girls mattered.

To our son Raj, many thanks over the years for reading and suggesting as these stories came alive. And to my husband, Gopal, who braved and conquered the complexities of Windows 11 at 2 a.m. when all seemed lost, there are not enough words for thank you, *shukria*.

Most writers can't publish their book without solid tech support, and I was blessed with Narinder Kumar, who helped with the website, photos, and advice on daily life in India. Also deep thanks to our daughter Jennifer Kirklin for her technical expertise and web design.

In memory of Sid Salinger, the best scribe in a family of noted writers, who re-woke the writer in me through critiques that often began with, "You've done it again!" His words still make my spirits soar.

"We owe a lot to the Indians, who taught us how to count, without which no worthwhile scientific discovery could have been made."
Albert Einstein

About the Author

I.D. Kapur majored in journalism and is a speech writer and prize-winning poet whose work is featured in the anthology, *Ink Spots*. She began traveling at seventeen to Europe and has visited over twenty countries. A year's stay in Northern India and over a dozen extended visits inspired her to write short stories based on her experiences. She lives in Northern California with her author husband.

Watch for her next book, *A Year Without Men,* in 2023.

Website:

www.idkapur.com

Made in the USA
Middletown, DE
26 October 2022

13506182R00130